BACKCOUNTRY BETTY

BACKCOUNTRY BETTY

JENNIFER WORICK

ILLUSTRATED BY KATE QUINBY

SKIPSTONE

Published by Skipstone, an imprint of The Mountaineers Books
Manufactured in the United States of America

First edition, 2007

Project Editor: Janet Kimball
Copy Editor: Joeth Zucco
Cover Design: Kate Basart
Book Design and Layout: Mayumi Thompson
Illustrations: Kate Quinby
Cover illustration: Kate Quinby

Library of Congress Cataloging-in-Publication Data
Worick, Jennifer.
  Backcountry Betty : roughing it in style / Jennifer Worick.—1st ed.
     p. cm.
  ISBN-13: 978-1-59485-070-7 (ppb)
  1. Outdoor recreation. 2. Women—Recreation. I. Title.
  GV191.64.W67 2007
  796.082—dc22
                                        2007023787
ISBN 13: 978-1-59485-070-7

Skipstone books may be purchased for corporate, educational, or other
promotional sales. For special discounts and information, contact our Sales
Department at 1-800-553-4453 or mbooks@mountaineersbooks.org.

Skipstone
1001 SW Klickitat Way
Suite 201
Seattle, Washington 98134
206-223-6303
www.skipstonepress.org
www.mountaineersbooks.org

♻ Printed on recycled paper

LIVE LIFE. MAKE RIPPLES.

CONTENTS

ACKNOWLEDGMENTS

This book wouldn't exist without the help of many creative, rugged, and imaginative folks. I first have to thank my patient, knowledgeable, and kind editor Dana Youlin, who helped move the manuscript from primitive to polished. I have to thank Editor-in-Chief Kate Rogers, who originally thought up the idea of *Backcountry Betty*, for putting the project in my manicured hands. And then there's the rest of the team, who brought this adorable and handy book into creation: designers Kate Basart and Mayumi Thompson, illustrator Kate Quinby, project editor Janet Kimball, copy editor Joeth Zucco, and proofreader Lynn Greisz.

My life coach Elizabeth Hechtman has been invaluable in helping me to grow as a writer and person, and my agent Joy Tutela has been a tremendous support, whether in the middle of contract negotiations or dishing about a favorite reality show (which I'm not ashamed to say I'd miss if I were camping). Über capable in or out of the asphalt jungle, I'd be happy to have them join me on a camping trip any time, any where.

In addition to my Brownie troop, my band of Betties—Alison Rooney, Sacha Adorno, Laurel Rivers, Liz Jones, Gina Johnston, Janet Basas Lipinski, Amy Walker, Kerry Colburn, Kerry Sturgill, Melissa McDaniels, Larissa Webb—taught me a thing or two about communing with nature without sacrificing style or hygiene. In particular, Elise Ballard Gilbert knows her way around a camp stove and she generously shared her expertise and recipes with me. Melissa Loden and her kin love to go camping with ease and style as much as possible, and she divulged all the tips she's learned over the years.

To varying degrees, my family enjoys rustic life, national parks, cooking and eating alfresco, and exploring the backcountry. Thank you all for taking me along on the trail, even if I went kicking and screaming and reapplying lip gloss at times.

And I have to thank my handsome Hugh, who kept me going through all of this. He helped me find my way out of the wilderness, even without a compass.

INTRODUCTION:
ROUGHING IT IN STYLE

I'm a Betty, and I'm proud of it. I wear my fashionista-diva-urban glamazon persona like a stylish badge of honor. Maybe it's because I never earned any Girl Scout badges when I was younger. Until a few years ago, I couldn't tell the difference between ivy and poison ivy, but I could pick out a certain designer's garment at 50 yards . . . without my serious prescription eyeglasses.

But something changed. I live in Seattle. Whether I like it or not, I have to venture into the woods, meander along the shoreline, wade in the water, kayak in the Sound. And mostly I like it. Sometimes I even love it. But I haven't given up my Betty status. I just make sure I have an active-length manicure and a great moisturizer with SPF. Oh, and I wear a hat to protect my highlights. And carry loads of moist towelettes and hand sanitizer.

I sound high maintenance, don't I? Maybe so, but this probably sounds familiar too. See, I'm not the only Betty to explore the backcountry! Years ago, I went white-water rafting with some college friends. I figured I should open myself up to new experiences, just like I did when I got that ill-advised Brazilian. . . . Anyway, I came with all the gear the rafting outfitter recommended: river sandals, nylon shorts, bathing suit, change of clothes, sunscreen, water bottle, snacks, Trident gum (okay, I added the last item). My friend Janet came with a full

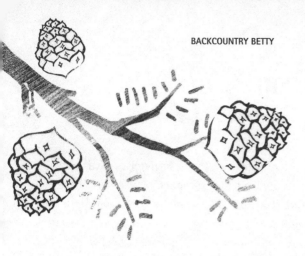

make-up kit and sported an active-length acrylic manicure she got for the occasion. She even got a French manicure so she would blend in with the locals.

Amy brought electric curlers.

I had three thoughts. One, who was she trying to impress in Albright, West Virginia? We were sleeping in a converted school filled with bunk beds and other grimy rafters. Two, the river and the helmets would probably do in any hairdo she might create. Three, where was she going to plug in? While I thought them a bit extreme in their girliness, I also sympathized with Janet when she broke a nail falling out of the raft. I tried to talk up Amy's sleek, straight, flat coif at the end of the day (she quickly transformed it into a French twist). Looking good is important to women, no matter where we might find ourselves.

I was dating a guy with a pilot's license and flew with him for a three-day folk festival in upstate New York. Some might not consider sleeping in a tent and sporadic showering roughing it. For me, it was like journeying into the Middle Ages. All I could think about was hygiene. I loaded up with Handiwipes, Wetnaps, Purell, bottles of water, bronzer, sunscreen, hats, beef jerky, and my knitting bag. I had no idea what the plumbing would be like, I feared the food would be vegan, and I was prepared to be bored by many of the acts.

In Betty's Backpack

Proper footwear and attire

First-aid kit (see page 128)

Repair kit with pocketknife (see page 159)

Sunscreen

Ibuprofen

Ziploc bags and plastic bags

Headlamp or flashlight (for nighttime manicures or reading *Vogue*) and extra batteries and bulbs

Sports watch (please, leave the Cartier at home)

Compass (learn how to use it before you leave home)

Trail map

Moist towelettes

Hand sanitizer

Small travel bottles for your key toiletries (hair straightening balm and lip plumper don't qualify), such as cleanser, moisturizer, sunscreen

Insect repellent (Avon's Skin-So-Soft is a classic way to smell good *and* ward off mosquitoes)

Waterproof matches or a lighter

If you have space (and I'd recommend you make room)

Cotton balls/pads (which double as firestarter)

Leave-in conditioner

Powder shampoo

Liquid soap (especially if there are facilities nearby with running water)

Anti-perspirant, natural deodorant

Battery-operated vibrator (okay, maybe this isn't exactly necessary, but you might be glad you packed it)

Discuss with your campanions who's bringing the shared gear: tent, sleeping bags, camp stove, cooler, cooking gear, can opener, corkscrew, food, etc. Distribute the weight evenly (that is, carry your water, trail mix, and sunscreen and leave the rest to him).

Jon and I got inventive, both in and out of the tent. We left the festival each day to explore a new swimming hole (*www.swimmingholes .org* was very helpful) and went a couple of times to a state park and swam in the lake. I felt pretty clean, even without shampooing my hair for a few days. Go figure. I got into the spirit of the adventure. With my Handiwipes tucked away in my cargo shorts, I was able to relax and enjoy the experience.

That's what *Backcountry Betty* is all about. It's an essential field guide that will allow the most polished of women to feel comfortable, put together, and capable during those times when they find themselves off the grid and, gasp!, out of cell phone range.

But as a Betty, you know the responsibility you have to keep the great outdoors, well, great. To that end, you must try to "leave no trace." In other words, leave the wilderness as close to pristine as you possibly can. While enjoying the outdoors, you should do everything possible to travel through it with the least impact. So can you be all fancy and girly when you have to worry about fluffing the grass behind you and packing out your used TP? .

Good question, even if you'd rather not think about such unpleasant topics. *Backcountry Betty* will cover the basics of ethical wilderness behavior and then push beyond that to show you how to make everything come up roses in the wild, even if things don't always exactly smell like roses, if you get my drift.

LEAVE NO TRACE

The LNT movement is pretty self-explanatory. There are a lot of tips and strategies when trekking into the wilderness, but the guiding principle is to leave as little impact or trace of yourself when you go on a hike, camping trip, kayaking excursion, rock climbing adventure, or any wilderness activity. This means walking on established trails, packing in and out all gear, food, and waste, and leaving wildlife be.

Multi-tasking your Glam Gear

The Betty staples that can serve another purpose in the wild.

Mirror: put in your contacts, signal for help, start a fire

Lipstick: rub on lips, use as firestarter smeared on cotton balls or tissue, mark a trail

Mouthwash: freshen breath, sterilize a wound

Moisturizer/lotion: hydrate and protect your skin, lubricate a stuck jar

Perfume: smell like flowers, sterilize a wound

Gum: freshen breath, secure a note to a trailhead

Blotting papers: absorb excess oil, write a note, crumple into tinder

Tweezers: pluck your eyebrows, pull out a sliver

Emery board: shape nails or file a downed stick to a point for a skewer

Nail polish: protect nails, cover a leak in a jacket or shoe, use as firestarter

Tissues: blow nose, wipe various body parts, use as napkins, crumple into tinder

Pill bottle: store matches, medication, and keys, turn into fishing lure

Lip gloss or lip balm with SPF: protect lips and if tinted, rub into cheeks as blush, can be used as firestarter when smeared on cotton balls

LEAVE NO TRACE PRINCIPLES

1. Plan ahead and prepare.
2. Travel and camp on durable surfaces (and I don't mean sidewalks).
3. Dispose of waste properly, no matter how unsavory the thought.
4. Leave what you find—take a picture instead.
5. Minimize campfire impacts.
6. Respect wildlife. That bear cub may look warm and fuzzy, but its mother isn't.
7. Be considerate of other visitors, even if they don't display the same grace and breeding.

Chapter 1
......

FIRST THINGS FIRST:
HYGIENE

I don't know about you, but it's hard for me to focus on the task at hand or the fun in the forest unless I've got my toilette taken care of and odor issues under control. There's nothing worse than feeling the deodorant evaporating or dripping under your arms on a hot day. And I'm not as fit as I'd like to be so my thighs stick slightly to each other as I trudge along. Yuck. Of course, this is to be expected during a rigorous hike or kayaking excursion, but that doesn't mean you don't want to start out fresh and then, at the end of your day's exertions, clean yourself up before climbing into your sleeping bag.

Or maybe it's just me.

I didn't think so.

Betties have long been challenged by hygiene outside of civilization. The Porta-Potties at that outdoor concert last summer left you emotionally scarred. I know, sweetie. I was the one standing in line next to you desperately looking for a Kleenex in my handbag and hoping my quads wouldn't give out as I squatted over the gaping pee hole.

Let us never speak of it again. No band is worth breathing through your mouth for that long.

But as damaging to the spirit as a makeshift bathroom can be, you will have to face this and more on the trail. In all likelihood, there will be no pre-existing toilet or hole or toilet paper or ability to flush. And get this, you'll need to pack out your used TP. Ziploc bags and Handiwipes. It's all about the Ziplocs and Handiwipes.

Just focus on how magnificent your surroundings are and how great the air smells when you aren't doing your business . . . and pack a buttload of Ziploc baggies.

So, how can you stay fresh as a daisy without cramming your bathroom counter (and the paper goods aisle at the drugstore) into your backpack? Travel-sized bottles are an excellent place to start, yes, but there are a few other tips you can keep in mind.

KEEPING CLEAN

The good news is that it's pretty easy to clean up in God's country. Not that long ago, Betties were stuck trying to make things work with bar soap and potable water that ran out far too quickly and really should have been saved for drinking. Today you don't have to choose between smelling like ass or dying of thirst. Save the water for cooking and drinking.

I'm a huge fan of moist towelettes, small bottles of hand sanitizer, and make-up remover and cleansing cloths. They all pack easily and are anything but messy. When you are done cleaning up, just pop the used wipe in a Ziploc bag to discard later when you return to civilization. And the hand sanitizer just dries by itself.

To save valuable packing space, pick products that do double duty. The beauty industry has come a long way in creating all-in-one shampoo/conditioner/body wash products that don't strip your hair or leave an oily film on your skin. Just be sure to check the label before lathering up with a zesty liquid soap. You don't want a dry, itchy scalp when you are far away from a drugstore or your favorite beauty counter.

DON'T BURST THE BUBBLE

Whether or not you are in civilization or the wilderness, you should always refrain from popping any pimples or picking at acne and blemishes. Sanitary conditions are grim, so your risk of irritating or infecting the inflamed area is higher. It gets dark quickly in the wilderness so your campanions probably won't even notice your third eye, even though you feel that it's blinking, winking, and otherwise attracting attention.

If you simply cannot stand having the pimple pulsing (it feels like it has its own heartbeat!) on your face, use hand sanitizer on your hands and let it dry. Press a warm compress (dip a cloth in warm, clean water) over Rudolph's nose/the stoplight/Mount St. Helens. Then place an index finger on either side. Take your time, as you probably don't have a mirror handy (but you could try looking at your reflection in a calm pool of water). Now gently pull *away* from the blemish with both fingers. If it doesn't pop, leave it alone. Apply a cold compress (dip a cloth in cold, clean water and apply to reduce redness and swelling). You can apply a tinted blemish stick to the area—it will calm and cover.

• • • • • • • • • • • Cleaning Up without Water • • • • • • • • • • •

Face cleansing cloths, soapless cleanser that can be rubbed into skin or wiped off without water (such as Cetaphil), astringent/toner with cotton pads

Hair powder shampoo, braid or put in a bandanna and let it go

Body moist towelettes, hand sanitizer (keep it away from your privates, as it's alcohol-based)

Feet antiseptic spray, foot powder (sprinkle lightly to avoid creating an unpleasant foot paste)

WHEN NATURE CALLS

You may be a lady, but you're also human. This means that you will have to relieve yourself at some point on the trail. Discretion and safety are still to be had. Let's get the big stuff out of the way.

Building a Cat Hole

If you've selected your spot to set up camp for the night, you need to dig a cat hole or latrine for your elimination needs. No, I don't know why it's called a cat hole. I've thought about it, but the options are just too disturbing. Regardless of its etymology, a cat hole is, well, a hole you dig in the ground. Because you're doing your business in this hole, you should locate it well away from water (200 feet), trails, and your campsite, preferably downwind.

But practicality and Betty beauty are not mutually exclusive. Even with the guidelines, pick a spot with a great, secluded view that isn't going to be too challenging when it comes time to drop trou. If you haven't been working on your quads with your trainer and can't squat for long, build the hole near a branch, tree, or log that you can grab onto while doing your business.

Once you find your prime real estate, using a small trowel or shovel, dig a hole that's four to eight inches deep and four to six inches wide. You're ready to go.

If you are roughing it somewhere that lacks wooded seclusion, such as the desert or beach, look for a deserted area and build a cat hole, remembering to clean up after yourself. As far as peeing in a pond or other body of water, *don't*. Swimming is fine but anything more can upset the ecosystem, and in the ocean, you can attract the attention of sharks. Also, avoid going into deep salt water if you are menstruating. Sharks have scary olfactory senses, and can detect blood and urine from far distances. If having your period wasn't bad enough, a visit from a shark would definitely put a damper on your outing. I've seen *Jaws* enough times to be afraid (but frankly, once would have sufficed).

Love Your Latrine

The Leave No Trace movement generally encourages cat holes over large latrines, since it spreads your waste in small spaces over a large area. But if you have a large group that's camping for several days, it might make sense to make one latrine for the group, rather than sending campers off into the woods with a trowel each time they need to poo.

Again, scout out a location 200 feet away from the campsite and any water sources. Dig a rectangular hole at least a foot deep (and wider than it is deep). If you have a large enough group (meaning, if you have cars and campers to pack in gear), bring a toilet seat to put over the hole.

After each use, instruct campers to throw some soil in the hole. When the waste rises to just four or six inches from the edge of the hole, cover the hole and dig another latrine.

• •

TIP: Drink plenty of water while you're out and about. If you become dehydrated, you run the risk of diarrhea, not exactly what you want in the woods.

Assuming the Position

Whether or not you'll have a toilet seat or simply a hole when doing your business, you'll most likely want to squat. Spread your legs, roll up your pant leg (if you are wearing pants), and drop trou. Try to keep your pants or shorts above your knees as you pee or poop. Hopefully, you built your cat hole or latrine near a tree or shrub (no poisonous or rash-inducing flora, please!) that you can hold onto for support if you need to squat for some time.

When you are done, do a little shake to get as much liquid off as possible. You know what I'm talking about. Then clean up with a towelette and stuff it into a Ziploc bag. Carry your trash with you to dispose of later.

● ●

> **TIP:** If you are fearful of going off the trail by yourself, ask your campanion to go with you and keep watch with his back to you while you do your business. When you are done, turn your baggie inside out, slip it over your hand, and use it as a glove of sorts to pick up your used TP. Flip the bag right side out and seal it. In lieu of toilet paper or towelettes, you can use found items to clean up. Seaweed, moss, leaves, and even snow can be used and then buried in the cat hole with your waste.

GOING WITH THE FLOW

Hopefully, you will anticipate your period and not be caught empty-handed when it shows up deep in the forest. Pack a Ziploc bag with pads or tampons and bring along another Ziploc for your used items. You will have to portage (a fancy word for carry) those until you find a proper disposal receptacle. They may be biodegradable but that will take a long time and the scent will attract wildlife. Add a perfumed towelette, crushed aspirin, or used tea bag to the used bag to stave off any odor.

And when it comes to PMS and feeling queasy and cranky (for reasons other than the monster incline you are traversing), there are some natural remedies you can jump on. Endorphins can actually alleviate your premenstrual pain, so a vigorous hike or kayaking outing can lift your spirits (hard to believe, but that serious grade you're hiking up will take your mind off your PMS, if not lessen the pain). A lovely sunny day can help matters. Herbal teas containing St. John's Wort can address your symptoms. I find that sharp smells like rosemary, pine, and peppermint lift my spirits and take my mind off of my cramps, nausea, and depression, not to mention the pissedoffedness I feel about being somewhere other than planted on my couch watching TV. Of course, packing a handful of Motrin in a corner of your butt pack is a surefire way to ensure that you don't turn into a bitchy Betty.

Reining in PMS

I know, some of these tips seem a bit extreme. I mean, how are you supposed to forego salt on the rim of your margarita, let alone pass up the margarita? But extreme pain calls for extreme measures.

✧ Eat small, frequent meals   ✧ Dial down the fatty foods

✧ Avoid caffeine and alcohol   ✧ Reduce sugar and salt intake

✧ Munch on trail mix, fruit, veggies

THE SPONGE BATH

I know you like your huge tub and your ridiculously pricey showerhead, but they aren't exactly practical when you're on the move and soaking up your rustic surroundings. So what's a Betty to do?

Embrace the sponge bath, that's what. Water is a precious commodity so resist the urge to rinse shampoo out of your hair with all of your potable drinking water. If there is any sort of stream, river, or lake, use your surroundings to your advantage and take a refreshing dip. Do not use any bar, liquid soap, or shampoo of any kind, even if you scored free samples of your favorite body soufflé or gelee at a fancy beauty boutique. Leave them in your bathroom to enjoy when you get back home and strip off your gamey gear. Instead, after taking a swim, run a damp washcloth or moist towelette over your skin and pop it into a plastic bag when done.

Pat yourself dry with an absorbent towel; if it's chilly out, well, that's another story. Heat up some water on your Coleman stove or campfire (boil it to kill any bacteria if you're a germaphobe), but let it cool to a reasonable temperature before giving yourself a good slap and tickle.

. . . .

TIP: It's fine to bathe in bodies of water, as long as you don't use soap (call it wading, taking the waters, or swimming if it makes you feel better). Wear your clothes if you want to freshen up your garments at the same time.

FIGHTING THE DREADED B.O.

There are few two-letter combinations that strike dread into the heart of a Betty the way B and O can (even BM—bowel movement—and SO—sold out—don't quite measure up). You probably thought certain smells could never roll off your body. Well, Betty, we can't always smell like flowers or baby powder or a certain herb that can only be harvested during the last two weeks in July. So what's a girl to do when she finds herself huffing and puffing on an uneven trail—as if that's not bad enough!—only to catch a whiff of something sharp and pungent rising like steam all around her?

I know, sweetie. It makes me slightly ill, too.

While many wilderness guides recommend going without any sort of deodorant or scent, I can't fully subscribe to the practice. I endorse the Leave No Trace ethic, I do. But I believe in the Avoid Self-Disgust philosophy as well.

For a natural remedy, rub a sprig of rosemary under your armpits to eliminate body odor and perk up your mood. Wear clothing that allows your skin to breathe and wicks away moisture from your body. There are even fabrics that contain antibacterial agents to cut down on odor and germs. Polypropylene, MTS 2, and Capilene are all fabrics designed to wick away moisture; check the label for information about the garment's odor-control properties. Outerwear, underwear, and all outdoor clothing made with these fabrics are a great investment, as they make you feel more comfortable and slightly less grody.

But before you worry about your outerwear stinking, consider your own aroma. Deodorant, while a lovely thing, can actually attract mosquitoes and bears so you might consider, gasp, going sans your Lady Speedstick for a couple of days, or opting for an antiperspirant only. If you are able to wash up somewhat with a sponge bath and towelettes and have fresh clothes, you won't faint from self-loathing. And if it gets really bad, try breathing through your mouth for a while. Forget about all the breathwork you've been doing in your yoga practice. If you don't breathe through your nose, you won't smell yourself or anyone else. Of course, you won't be able to stop and smell the flowers, either.

If you are at any sort of campsite or have access to running water or public showers, consider showering at night to avoid the rush of early-bird nature enthusiasts. Doing this will help you relax before turning in and you'll avoid stinking up your bedroll. And if you know there are shower facilities and indoor plumbing where you'll be camping, stop for a moment of silent gratitude and pack all the travel-sized lotions and potions you can carry, along with your toothbrush and toothpaste, in a Ziploc bag you can easily tote to and from your camp.

- -

> **TIP:** Rock crystal deodorants are great alternatives to mainstream deodorants and anti-perspirants. They are made from mineral salts and are fragrance free, which will hold off enthusiastic mosquitoes. Just moisten the crystal and rub it under your arms.

DON'T STAND SO CLOSE TO ME

You've been hiking or kayaking or ziplining all freakin' day. And you're bone tired. But you suddenly realize that things can get worse, and they just did. You sniff the air only to find the foul odor that attracted your attention is coming from your mouth. You've got a case of halitosis, the likes of which haven't been seen since seventh grade when Todd Moody tried to kiss you at a dance in the cafeteria. But this time, it's much, much worse. This time, you're the one with the smell of decay coming out of your mouth.

There are a few options to rejoin the land of the living. You can always choose to steer clear of people, but where's the fun in that?

Chew coarse foods, for one. I know Betty likes her mac and cheese, but it and other "smooth" foods (sadly, cheese and chocolate fondue) are a surefire way to develop bad breath. Instead, when you sit down to eat, try to chow on coarser foods, like salad and vegetables. They act as natural tongue scrapers, eliminating or reducing the amount of bacteria in your mouth.

Other things to do include squirreling away gum and breath mints (although gum can increase gas production in the Betty body), or chewing on orange rinds, parsley, cinnamon sticks, and cloves. Oh, and flossing really is important in moving the bacteria along so pack a tiny spool of it in your toiletry bag. You don't want that beef jerky to get stuck in your molars.

HOT LIPS

Armed with your Betty checklists, there's no way you forgot your lip balm with SPF. But maybe you lost it when you flipped your kayak or used it up after a dusty day in the sun. Whatever the case, your lips need some protection and moisture. This is the time to turn to food, and not just from depression. Olive oil, honey, and even the beeswax from an unscented candle or comb honey can be used to protect your lips. In fact, these are ingredients that are often used in lip and body products. You can also carefully apply a small amount of sunscreen lotion to your mouth, but refrain from licking your lips, kissing, or otherwise consuming the product.

KEEPING GAS UNDER WRAPS

If you are really embracing the spirit of your outdoor adventure, it might be time to just let it rip when you are feeling particularly gassy. Seeing as you are in a wide open space, your gas will quickly dissipate. However, if you're in close quarters in a tent or just can't bring yourself to unclench your sphincter, try drinking some peppermint tea or even chewing on some peppermint, an herb that settles your stomach. When you use the latrine or visit a cat hole, use the alone time to get as much gas out of your system as possible. This will buy you some time when in the company of others.

To prevent the dreaded fart, eat small meals and snacks, limit your dairy (probably not hard if you're camping without much in the way of refrigeration), avoid soda and carbonated beverages (yes, even the tonic in your cocktail counts), don't chew gum, and steer clear of the pork and beans. You know you'll probably have gas at some point during your excursion, but why tempt fate?

Chapter 2
......

GETTING YOUR GLAM ON IN THE AMAZON

*L*ooking like a rock star while collecting rocks, leaves, and wildflowers isn't always possible, nor is it recommended. While I always like to stand out in a crowd, I think it more important to look appropriate. So just like I wouldn't wear a ball gown to a ball game, I wouldn't wear silly sandals or anything that needs to be dry-cleaned when I'm "experiencing nature."

That said, you don't have to go completely down the fleecy rabbit hole and trick yourself out with shapeless sweatshirts and colorless lip balm. It's a slippery slope and letting yourself go in one area can snowball until you are a wooly mountain woman who people steer clear of, as much for your appearance as for your natural odor.

I don't mean to scare you, but looking fabulous takes a little work. No matter how "natural" that glowing actress appears, don't be fooled. It takes a lot of work/artifice/people to look that natural. Self-tanner, bronzer, hair cream and hair elastics, and pricey but perfect-fitting tanks are but a few of the easier solutions to looking natural but add to that trips to the dermatologist for peels, trips to the allergist for shots, and ugly, ugly hiking boots and you get some idea of the sacrifices you must make to look like you are a natural on the trail. Are you thoroughly freaked out? Good. I wanted to emphasize the point so you don't take it lightly and underpack, stuffing only sunscreen and deodorant into your, gulp, backpack.

So how can you look appropriate and stylish while being somewhat wild-ish? The first key to beauty is your attitude. If you are enjoying breathing fresh air and taking in the flora and fauna, your bright-eyed and bushy-tailed demeanor will make you glow. Part of that attitude is treating your backroads adventure like a spa experience. This is a chance to clean out your pores with fresh air and minimal makeup, tighten up your glutes with some serious switchbacks, and work your magic away from the maddening crowds.

•••••••••••• **It's All How You Look at It** ••••••••••••

Your outdoor adventure may seem grimy and icky but it's really how you view it. Whether you feel the need to make excuses for your scummy appearance to others or yourself, here's how to see your trip in a less-grody light.

Rash	"It's the result of a chemical peel."
Mosquito bite	"Oh that. It's a hickie (or beauty mark). Yes, on my thigh."
Sunburn	"I always burn before I tan. It's my burden and my gift."
Sweaty brow	"Flushed, glowy skin is in, haven't you heard?"
Body odor	"It's no worse than post-cardio-funk class." "I'm flushing out toxins."
Matted, greasy hair	"Dirty hair makes updos easier to manage."
Cargo shorts	"These are the greatest inventions ever! The pockets hold lip gloss, cuticle cream, hair elastics, my sleep mask, sunscreen. . . . I need a pair for going out in the city."
Scratch	"Oh, I got a little carried away last night . . . if you get my drift."
Blisters	"The same thing happened when I broke in my red Manolos."

YOUR GROOMING GUIDE

Before you go off collecting pinecones, making out against a tree, or otherwise communing with nature, there are a few measures you can take to free yourself from the worry that comes from not being able to check yourself out in a mirror. Instead, you'll be free to worry about strange noises and the possibility of a bear lumbering across your path.

Advance planning works for NASA and brides, so why shouldn't it work for you? The best piece of advice that I can offer is to plan ahead. Assuming you are aware of your upcoming trip into the wild, you can arrange for a bit of grooming before you hit the trail.

Now a word about some specific grooming activities:

BODY HAIR: Waxing isn't the most comfortable of spa treatments but is probably the most useful for a quick or lengthy trip to the woods. In addition to your normal eyebrow and bikini waxing, consider waxing your leg, underarm, and lip (just schedule it all for at least a week prior to the trip to avoid any rashes or reactions). You'll feel sleek as a seal and that feeling will carry through your off-road adventure. Waxing your bikini area will make you feel slightly fresher, or maybe that's just me. And just wait until your guy rubs his hand over your leg, only to find it soft and smooth, no stubble in sight. He'll wonder if he's dreaming. He's not, but you are downright dreamy.

MANICURES AND PEDICURES: Every Betty loves her mani/pedis. Get a pedicure before you go, seal with a topcoat, and enjoy the sight of your polished toes throughout your excursion. Paint them a bright color; it adds a touch of glam to the event. Your fingers are another story. You'll be using your hands a lot, and chances are you'll chip even the best manicure during the first day. So opt for a nice buffing or a clear strengthening polish instead (and you can pack an all-in-one tool that files and buffs if you need to touch up during the trip) and leave the dragon red polish at home.

PERMANENT MAKEUP/TATTOO: This is one case where you might want to step away from the esthetician and get some perspective. Unlike a Brazilian, this is a treatment you'll have to live with long after your rustic weekend is over. Michael Jackson and his perma-eyeliner

Your Wilderness Grooming Schedule

1 month prior

⟡ Wrap your mind around the idea that you won't have any indoor plumbing

⟡ Start making lists of products you'd like to bring along and then start editing the list down, opting for products that don't require water

1 week prior

⟡ Wax your bits and pieces (doing this too close to your trip can result in skin irritation)

⟡ Exfoliate both face and body

⟡ Apply self-tanner daily

⟡ Avoid products with retinol or alpha-hydroxy acids until after your trip (mixing retinol and AHA products can irritate your skin if you are exposed to a lot of sun)

1 day prior

⟡ Deep cleanse your skin and apply a hydrating masque

⟡ Color or highlight your hair (make sure to pack a hat so you can protect your color from the sun)

⟡ Shampoo and deep condition your hair (if not coloring)

⟡ Do a final plucking of eyebrows and shaving of underarms and legs

⟡ Give yourself a pedicure, taking care to slough off dead skin and slather lotion onto your feet

⟡ Buff your fingernails

⟡ Pack your favorite products in travel-sized containers and in Ziploc bags should be a cautionary tale. Wear sunglasses instead, and hide your eyes altogether.

TANNING AND BRONZING: There's good news for the lily-white gals out there. Self-tanners have come a long way since the orange streaks of QT. I remember one particularly bad experiment involving QT, Sun-In, a lawn chair, and a boom box playing a Duran Duran cassette. Good times, bad results. Today, you can buy lotions and potions for your natural skin tone that will build a slight tan over a week. Wash your hands and avoid putting on clothing until it dries or you'll still get junior high results. There are also spray-on tans that you can do yourself or have a professional airbrush on you. You are sprayed with a bronzer that has self-tanner in it. After a day of a lovely molten glow, wash the bronzer off, and you're left with a tan that will last you throughout your entire trip, unless you plan on walking the Appalachian Trail, in which case you're on your own. There are always tanning booths, which I tend to avoid since I burned myself badly right before prom. You could opt for a liquid or powder bronzer, but I don't recommend it. If you are perspiring, it could streak or cake up and just make you look dirty. And without a decent mirror, it's difficult to determine if you even applied it properly in the first place.

HAIR: Ah, our crowning glory. In the wilderness, it could become a crowning gory story. Just because you're deep in the forest doesn't mean you have to adopt the look of Jodie Foster in *Nell*. Please. I'm not talking about an elaborate updo. A clean ponytail is often enough to keep your hair out of your face and you looking sleek.

If you color your hair regularly, schedule an appointment before your trip. Since you are often admonished not to wash your hair for several days after the processing anyway, here's a perfect chance to let your hair go unwashed with purpose. But be sure to wear a hat. If you are in the sun, the color could fade prematurely. Carry a hat that works with your hairdo—a high ponytail doesn't work with a bucket hat, for instance. Switch to a baseball cap, or rock pigtails with the bucket hat. A sleek ponytail or pigtails will reduce your chance of hat head. Also consider tucking away a wide cloth headband or bandanna. It will keep your hair back à la Jackie O, and it's perfect when you need to wash your face. You can also channel your inner Olivia Newton-John when you get physical by tying your headband across your forehead.

If you don't color your hair, this is still a perfect time to get a haircut and professional blowout. Explain to your stylist that you'll probably be wearing a hat for a few days. He or she will give you a sleek blowout that will still look chic after a hard day's hike.

In lieu of showering and washing your hair, use the power of nature to your advantage. I once explored lakes and swimming holes as a means of keeping my coif fresh. I didn't take my shampoo. I figured that if I simply *had* to wash my hair, rinsing my hair in fresh water would be enough to get me by, and it was. I wrapped my hair around my index finger and made corkscrew curls while my hair was damp. As it dried, it produced the most ravishing pre-Raphaelite, wood nymphy locks. And soft waves are easy to twist into a French twist or pull back into a high pony. You can also braid your damp hair for crimped waves. But just like Joan Crawford eschewed wire hangers, so too should every Betty reject scrunchies. If you have long hair, pack plenty of elastics and put them in different pockets so you won't lose all of them at once.

And don't turn your nose up at powder shampoos. Even high-end salon lines have come a long way. When you feel your hair getting a bit gamey, sprinkle the shampoo through your locks. The powder absorbs any oil and refreshes your do.

TIP: Use your shampoo as a body wash (but not vice versa). Use a light lotion as a hair conditioner in a pinch.

TIP: When humidity and heat do a doozy on your do, run a dollop of sunscreen through your locks to tame flyaways and protect your hair color from fading in the sun.

SKIN CARE ON THE GO

Your skin will need additional care during your adventure. Sun, sweat, flora, and fauna all go to work on your skin, and the results can be as rough as tree bark. While fresh air is delightful and a week without makeup can clear out your pores, unwashed, sunburned skin with what looks to be a nasty rash is anything but desirable.

A little goes a long way and you don't have to pack your medicine cabinet to look and feel 100 percent Betty.

When it comes to your skin, there are a lot of products cramming the drugstores that you can creatively pack in your gear. Even if you have a strapping lad to carry your stuff, wouldn't you rather he carry cocktails and snacks?

As far as your face goes, pick up a tinted moisturizer with SPF. That way, you don't have to carry moisturizer, foundation, and sunscreen. You can also find a tinted lip balm with SPF (and yes, there are tinted, sparkly alternatives to Chapstik and Blistex). These can also double as a tint if you want to put some color in your cheeks, although I suspect hiking, pitching a tent, and rolling around in the aforementioned tent will give you a cheeky flush. No matter how addicted, avoid glosses as your hair and bugs can get caught in the goo. If it's really hot out, also leave your favorite lipstick at home. It could melt. You could get angry.

Let me just take a moment to further emphasize the importance of sunscreen, both for your face and your body, and perhaps your hair. Carrying a pack is bad enough, but imagine doing it with sunburned shoulders. Oh, the chafing, the chafing. . . . Or maybe you've been looking forward to making out with your scruffy man after a long day of hiking, and your face is the color of a cooked lobster. You won't be able to enjoy any stubble burn. You'll just have to ask him to gently slather on aloe vera or healing lotion. That's hot, but not in the way you anticipated.

As a Betty, bugs, well, *bug* me. While I enjoy looking at dragonflies, by and large, bugs are for the birds. Well, not literally. So to avoid them, I look to insect repellent, both natural and not-so-natural. That brings me to the wonder that is Skin-So-Soft. Introduced by Avon in 1962, SSS was originally marketed as a bath oil and is one of the country's best-selling bath oils to this day. Its distinctive herbal scent was later found to keep mosquitoes at bay while making limbs glisten. It smells great and spawned a whole product line for Avon, including an actual insect repellent.

• •

TIP: Store your toiletries (and anything scented) in a bear-proof canister when in grizzly country. Not to scare you, but many parks and outdoor info sources suggest not using anything scented at all. Apparently bears, like your Grizzly Adams boyfriend, love sweet-smelling ladies too.

REPURPOSE YOUR FOOD

While body oil is all well and good for your extremities, you certainly don't want to slather it on your face. In fact, you might want to *remove* gunk from your face. Even in the wild, you can whip up a face masque from a few natural ingredients.

Honey-Oat Mask

If you brought honey and oatmeal as part of your movable feast, you've got a great moisturizing and exfoliating mask. Just mix together two teaspoons of honey to one teaspoon of oatmeal, slather it on a clean face, leave on for 10 minutes, and then rinse off with water, following up with moisturizer (with SPF if it's daytime).

Moisturizing Avocado Mask

Hold back a bit of avocado when making guacamole. Mash a quarter of a ripe avocado for a normal-to-dry skin treatment. Spread it on your face and neck, leave on for 20 minutes, and rinse off.

Banana Hair Treatment

If you want to moisturize your hair, mash up a banana and finger comb it through your damp clean hair. Leave on for a half hour and rinse out for ultra-soft (but not greasy) locks.

BUTT PACKS FOR BETTY

Butt packs, backpacks, and Camelbaks, oh my. (No, I didn't say cameltoe.) After many years of being cold, soggy, and muddy, I've finally come around to the idea that dressing for the backcountry is very different than dressing in a civilized society. The rules are different. Suddenly, anything clean becomes formal wear and pants that zip off to convert to shorts are actually chic. Feeling a bit nauseous at the thought? That's to be expected. But these foreign-looking garments are actually stylish when lounging next to a pristine alpine lake or paddling through white water.

Let's go through a few basics and figure out how to Betty them up without sacrificing comfort.

Don't Fight the Fleece

Our journey into the wilderness begins with fleece. Sweet, delicious, evil fleece. Fleece and Polartec are so lovely and comforting that it's easy to overlook how shapeless and boring they can be.

Just don't forget the fact that a hoodie and baseball cap are not appropriate for a swanky dinner, a night at the opera, or your sister's wedding. Keep your sense of occasion about you at all times. And this particular occasion requires that you zip into a sweatshirt, pull on some cute shorts that were designed with women in mind (i.e., don't borrow your boy's cargo shorts), and strap on some river sandals or hiking boots.

It's okay. You can shudder in horror.

While this vision of yourself is not particularly fetching, it can have certain advantages, such as attracting strapping mountain men who profess to like a girl who doesn't wear makeup and can join in the fun, even if that means sitting by a campfire knocking back Jagermeister. But I digress. Let's talk about how to look stylish while dressing appropriately for the trail.

Bettify Your Wilderness Wardrobe

Depending on the weather and the terrain, you might find yourself in a tank top, shorts, and sandals or a thick fleece sweatshirt, thermal underwear, and hiking boots. Regardless of this, you can spruce up your look. If it's hot and you're anticipating being sweaty, a fitted tank top and shorts are the way to go. Rather than just a plain tee or tank, however, purchase one with a colorful design that you designate just for wilderness adventures (otherwise you might be tempted to mix it in with your normal wardrobe and be reluctant to get it dirty and sweaty hiking up a mountain). I once wore a green tee with a comment about Lake Erie and attracted all sorts of fellow Michigander attention as I hiked in Washington State. Your clothes can invite conversation so why not take advantage of that? You could also imprint a cool design or logo onto a tank top with the use of special iron-on transfer paper and your inkjet or laser printer. As far as shorts go, look for ones with several pockets (to hold your lip balm, mirror, hair elastics, etc.) that hit at a complimentary spot on your thigh. Bermudas are back in style, so if you can find a slim cut that doesn't make your legs look stubby, go for it. You need to try on a few pairs to figure out what suits your form and is functional as well. Avoid fabrics that need to be dry-cleaned, no matter how great your ass looks. And avoid pleated shorts. They might be comfortable but they also add 10 pounds. If anything, you want to look thinner for all your efforts.

Just like a good Mexican seven-layer dip, the key to dressing in rustic conditions is layering, particularly if it's cold. Just like you put a gloss over a lipstick over a lipliner, so too should you layer a water-repellent shell (if it's rainy) over a fleece hoodie over a long-sleeved thermal tee. A colorful hoodie or shell not only draws an admiring eye, it will alert hunters to your presence and help search teams locate you if you become hopelessly lost (which won't happen). It will also brighten the day and your complexion in a way that navy or loden green can't.

Now you can use a less-than-titillating garment as a backdrop for embellishment. Before you hit the trail, you can embroider or iron on an adorable design of a deer, a leafy branch, or a hiking boot. You can take a basic tee and cut out the neckline and make it a boatneck. Cut off a couple of inches of the sleeve at an angle and make it a cap-sleeved top. If you don't have the time or nimble fingers needed for such a project, just take an old paste brooch out of your jewelry box and use it as a zipper pull. If you happen to get lost, you can use the sparkly rhinestones to signal for help.

Weather can turn quickly and catch you unawares, without the aid of the Weather Channel. You might want to leave the leather and suede behind and opt instead for a microfiber, water-repellent shell or parka. Various manufacturers are realizing that legions of Betties are venturing into the woods and are making fashion-forward, body-conscious jackets, so there's no reason to suffer the ginormous, bulky parka that makes you look like the Michelin man. Even down jackets are now being made with attention to slimness. Try on a few jackets and make sure they hit your waist in a place that doesn't accentuate your hips/thighs/butt/pooch/fill in the blank.

When shopping for backcountry clothes, pay attention to three things:

Color: Does the hue do for you?

Fit: Does the garment fit you as well as your everyday clothes?

Function: Does it serve its purpose for your trip? After all, you probably won't wear it anywhere else.

Dressing to the Occasion

As a Betty, you are always careful to dress to the occasion, whether that means slipping into some cute capri pants and a striped sailor shirt for an afternoon of boating or your favorite little black dress and spectacular stilettos for a chi chi cocktail party. Okay, so maybe a weekend trek in the mountains isn't exactly the same thing, but the same consideration has to go into your wardrobe. A bikini doesn't play in the mountains, and conversely, you wouldn't pack a parka for a tropical paradise.

As you prep for your trip, ask yourself the following questions:

Are you going somewhere:
- Tropical?
- Arid?
- Mountainous?
- Wooded?

Is the weather report predicting:
- Rain?
- Snow?
- Drought?
- Perfect, sunny conditions?
- Low temperatures?
- High temperatures?

Are you going for:
- The day?
- Overnight?
- A weekend?
- A lengthy trip?

Taking into account the climate, weather report, and length of trip will allow you to pack appropriate and ample garments. REI has a great website *(www.REI.com)* with all sorts of helpful information to assist you in choosing the right clothes for your trip.

MOUNTAINS

Pack layers and pack for warmth, no matter how warm it feels at base camp. It may be the middle of summer, but it can get chilly or downright frigid at certain times of day or night in the mountains or woods.

- Thick wool or synthetic hiking socks
- Hiking boots
- Fleece shell
- Water-resistant down parka
- Insulated pants
- Underwear with moisture-wicking action (meaning it pulls sweat away from your body)
- Long- and short-sleeved shirts
- Wool or hi-tech synthetic hat that covers ears

JUNGLE

It's going to be hot and it's going to be humid, a sultry cocktail indeed. If you will be trekking through the jungle, you will also have to protect your limbs and feet from underbrush and various critters that scurry, slither, and flit about. Pack clothes that will cover your limbs but let your skin breathe.

- Brimmed hat to block sun
- Lightweight pants and shorts
- Lightweight long-sleeved garments
- Netting to wrap around face or body to prevent insect attacks
- Sturdy, closed-toe shoes or knee-high boots

- Walking stick
- Pants, shirts, underwear, and socks with serious wicking action to keep moisture away from the body as much as possible

DESERT

Unlike the jungle or the forest, the desert is going to be arid in addition to hella warm. This is great for a sauna when you are wrapped in a towel but not ideal when you are baking under the harsh sun. Rather, you pretty much want to look like a wrapped-up nomad. Pack plenty of sunscreen and clothes that will save your skin, while also keeping you cool.

- Scarf to tie around neck or head or nose and mouth should a sandstorm arise
- Hat or helmet to block sun
- Sturdy walking sandals, boots, or shoes
- Wool or synthetic hiking socks
- Lightweight, light-colored pants
- Lightweight, light-colored long-sleeved shirts
- Thin, insulated jacket for cold nights

BEACH AND WATER

Your biggest enemy in a tropical beach setting is the sun. Don't be so seduced by the idea of busting out your hot new bikini that you overlook packing garments that will protect you from the sun's harmful rays.

- Bathing suit (in a pinch, a black sports bra and panties can double as a swimsuit)
- Cover up (a large pareo is both stylish and useful, as you can wrap and tie it into a sarong, halter dress, or shoulder wrap as need be. It can even act as a thin beach blanket.)

- Hat with brim to shield your lovely complexion
- Tanks and tees
- Long-sleeved shirts and lightweight jackets
- Shorts
- Lightweight pants
- River sandals
- Sunscreen (not a garment, but necessary for covering and protecting your limbs)

A NOTE ABOUT FIBER: Cotton may be the fabric of our lives, but it is not always the best, most comfortable choice when packing for the outdoors. In some instances, opting for cotton clothing can result in hypothermia. When cotton gets wet, it stays wet, meaning that if you are in the water, get rained on, or sweat profusely, the cotton t-shirt you're sporting, while downright adorable, will not dry quickly and can become sodden and clammy. Synthetic fibers are to be embraced, not scoffed at, when it comes to outdoor gear. Look for yoga tanks, long underwear, shirts, pants, jackets, and parkas that repel water, wick away moisture, and dry quickly. And for heavier sweaters, socks, and the like, wool is a great option too, as it naturally repels water. You don't see any fluffy sheep drowning from being waterlogged, now do you?

ONE LAST THOUGHT: Leave jewelry and anything valuable at home. There is no reason to wear diamond studs or a Tiffany heart necklace while hiking the Pacific Crest Trail. As I've said, with any fashion, it's vitally important to look appropriate to the occasion and well, jewels are anything but fashionable in the backcountry (they are slightly ridiculous, in fact, which I know is hard to wrap your brain around). And it's rough out there; your chances of losing a bauble are high and the chances of finding it slim.

A TRICKED-OUT BETTY

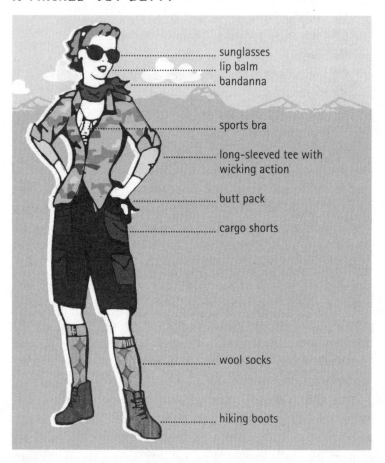

sunglasses
lip balm
bandanna

sports bra

long-sleeved tee with wicking action

butt pack

cargo shorts

wool socks

hiking boots

The Foot Path

You've most likely never given a whole lot of thought to your sock drawer and are thinking about just stuffing a few pairs of gym socks into your pack. Think again. All socks are not created equal, and you'll be a whole lot happier if you eschew the cotton tube socks or cute footsies for more appropriate outdoor socks. Think about the type of abuse your feet are going to take and then you can choose from a surprising number of thicknesses and fibers.

Sock liners are intended to be a buffer between your foot and thicker socks and to wick moisture away from your feet. Lightweight hiking socks provide wicking action but not as much warmth as thicker socks, making them comfortable for day hikes in warmer weather. Midweight socks are thicker, warmer, often padded to provide cushioning, and should be worn with liners. The thickest socks are mountaineering socks, which are designed for the long, cold haul. Wear them in cold, harsh conditions with liners.

And regarding fiber, put the cotton socks back in the drawer and reach for silk, wool, and synthetic fibers and materials (like polypropylene) that wick and insulate.

When it comes to footwear, as much care should go into your choice as when you were trying to find a pair of knockout kitten heels to match your new little black dress. Seriously. Again, assess whether you need lightweight boots for day hikes or durable boots for serious mountaineering excursions. Do you need waterproof or breathable materials? Nylon mesh is breathable and appropriate for day hiking in warm weather, whereas full-grain leather boots with waterproof barriers (like Gore-Tex) are made for serious wear in serious weather. How much tread is

necessary? Measure your feet properly and walk in the boots for a while before committing to a pair (finding out on the trail that your spiffy new boots rub against your ankle or heel is just as bad as the time you wrecked your feet dancing all night wearing four-inch stiletto boots). Look for shoes with few seams and a good connection between the upper and the sole (which is either stitched or cemented). Your feet, if not your fashion sense, will thank you.

Linger-Ley!

Ah, underwear. In the rush to assemble the perfect wilderness wardrobe, it's often easy to overlook the fact that you need sports bras, practical panties, and long underwear. No matter how saucy you want to feel under your fleece, don't pack the lacy confection of a bra and leave the thongs at home. Comfort is key, and you'll forget all about the desire to shock him in the tent with your custom-fitted corset after a hard day's journey into night.

If you have a large rack, well done. Buy a sturdy bra with wide straps and a thick band or underwire for maximum support. On the smaller side? You can probably get away with a sports bra top (some look like a tank or camisole with a built-in bra). No matter your cup size, look for nylon/spandex blends that wick away moisture, mesh inserts for ventilation, and flat seams that won't rub against your skin. Some bras even feature fabrics and finishes that help prevent odor-causing bacteria.

Title 9 Sports *(www.titlenine.com)* and Lucy *(www.lucy.com)* both offer a wide selection of sports bras for every size and activity, but if you can, it's always best to get fitted for one in person.

Believe me, Betty, you may not feel sexy strapping into your sports bra, but at the end of the day when you release your girls from their protective gear, you'll feel fantastic and your body will be ready to go.

As far as undies go, look for many of the same features: synthetic blends to wick away moisture, non-chafing seams and waistband, vents, odor-control features. For colder weather, go with long underwear. In warmer climes, opt for panties in your most comfortable cut.

CONSIDER THIS

If you think you can't go two days without your jacuzzi tub or salon products, remember this: I firmly believe you can make any adventure into a spa experience. True, you won't have the soothing sounds of nature being piped into the lavender-infused massage room, but you can get the real thing (save the massage table) when you venture into the backcountry. Here are a few ideas to get the juices flowing:

Slather your feet with an alpha-hydroxy or lactic acid lotion before pulling on your thick wool or snazzy moisture-wicking hiking socks and turning in for the night. Don't try to do this while hiking, as the slipperiness of your feet might cause more friction and therefore more blisters. Wait until you are idle to pamper your feet.

If you are near a beach, use the power of nature to exfoliate. Take off your sandals and walk or run through the sand. Combine it with a bit of water and rub it on your feet, elbows, and hands, or anywhere that might be a bit rough to the touch.

If you can find a smooth but thick stick lying about, place it on the ground and roll your arches over it for a quick foot massage.

River rocks or otherwise large smooth rocks that fit snugly into your palm can be used to give or receive a stone massage. If you can heat them in the sun, even better. With long, slow strokes, press the rock deeply into your back and leg muscles.

Breathe in the smell of lavender to relax or pine or rosemary to invigorate.

Create a makeshift venik (a bundle of dried oak branches that are soaked and then lightly beaten against the skin). If you can locate any oak or birch branches on the ground with dried leaves, soak them (overnight if you can). The belief is that when they are rewetted, the leaves release tannic acid that acts like an astringent to the skin. So when they are wet, beat your bare skin or someone else's skin with them.

The rain forest can act like a steam room of sorts, while the dry heat of the desert can provide the same effects of a sauna. Breathe in the wet or dry heat to clear out your lungs, and think, not that you are a sweating like a, uh, *murderer* in church, but rather that you are cleaning your pores and eliminating toxins.

Winter camping presents its own unique challenges, and the stark landscape can strain your eyes. So pack two tight, small snowballs and place them in a clean, dry sock liner. Lay over your eyelids to soothe your eyes.

Chapter 3
......

EATING OUT(SIDE)

Admit it: When you think about eating alfresco, surrounded by lush pines or sandy beaches, you think of hot dogs, s'mores, flapjacks. Mmm, a Betty knows how to stuff her piehole in a big way. And with the strength training and cardio you did all day (enough to shut up your hardcore personal trainer), you have every right to that fourth bratwurst.

And it probably tasted just as good as the first one. Fresh air and the great outdoors work up an appetite and just about anything, even beef jerky, tastes pretty darn good going down. But you don't necessarily have to sacrifice your fancy food standards when you are away from your chef's kitchen and fistful of takeout menus. True, it might not be a wise use of space to pack Xanthan gum or a bottle of precious saffron in your pack, even if you did pick up some killer techniques from *Top Chef*. But with a lot of forethought and minimal gear, you can whip up some snacklets that will have your campanions wondering how on earth you were able to squirrel away your personal chef.

And it doesn't have to take a lot of effort, either. You don't have to marinate for hours, wait for dough to rise, slow cook a hunk of meat (although that sounds damn good). You might eat your left arm while waiting for your pot roast, and who wants that? A little advance preparation when you set up your campsite will result in a serviceable and safe outdoor kitchen.

Game Time

As a Betty, you probably won't have much of a problem with this, but in the wild you should not hunt or otherwise disturb the wildlife. Keeping the Leave No Trace ethic in mind, going into the wilderness doesn't translate into hunting wild game or fishing. While a Betty might watch Bobby Flay on *Iron Chef America*, she's not going to be flaying or filleting anything anytime soon. You could, of course, if you *had* to, but let's save that skill for another day and focus on whipping up some culinary delights in the open air.

BEFORE YOU LEAVE YOUR KITCHEN

All camping cooks agree: Do as much advance prep at home as possible. Using small airtight plastic containers and Ziploc bags, chop and grind and pour and cook as many ingredients or dishes as you can before you leave your tricked-out kitchen. You want to do as little as possible at a rustic campsite when your fingers aren't exactly sterile.

Your *mise en place* should be completely set before you leave. To that end:

- Precook bacon (everything's better with bacon)
- Blanch vegetables like asparagus and green beans
- Parcook rice
- Brown meat
- Grind and premix spices (although everything should ideally be freshly ground, spices will keep for a few days just fine in baggies)

- 🍎 Make a killer dressing/marinade: Fill a small container with ¾ cup olive oil, ¼ cup red wine vinegar, 3 tablespoons of Dijon mustard, 3 chopped anchovies
- 🍎 Cut lemons in quarters and take with you (great for food and cocktails)
- 🍎 Chop and cut all vegetables that will stay crisp in an airtight container
- 🍎 Cook pasta: pop in cold water before putting it in a resealable container
- 🍎 Clean whole potatoes: put in oven for 20 minutes, let cool to room temperature and pop into a resealable container. At the campsite, you can cut into eight chunks and fry up on a flat surface or cook in heavy-duty foil with oil or butter.

Some things, however, can't be chopped or prepped without risking spoilage or just overall ickiness: avocadoes turn brown, tomatoes will go bad more quickly, basil will wilt. If you are planning on cooking up some fish, have your fishmonger cut it and just leave it alone until you are ready to prepare it.

Plan out your meals before you go. Pack foods in the order of when you plan to eat them, packing the most perishable items on top. While many ingredients can be used in different ways, it's helpful to think about which things should be eaten first for freshness and which foodstuffs will keep until the last day. Base your quantities on what you think each person can eat. For instance, if your man eats for two on a normal day, think about what he can put away when he's been hiking for six hours. Scary thought, isn't it?

And while it isn't a bad idea to carry some measuring cups and spoons, cooking outdoors should be an inexact science. You most likely aren't going to attempt a soufflé or chocolate ganache cake deep in the woods, so just eyeball quantities and season to taste. The fresh air and ravenous appetites make everything taste four-star.

Some foodstuffs that can be used in myriad ways:

- Onions and garlic: chop, slice, or mince and bring in large quantities
- Dried mushrooms or sundried tomatoes can be reconstituted and added to many things (sundried tomatoes are heavenly with tuna, for instance)
- Marinated artichokes
- Olives
- Lemons
- Take and reheat leftovers such as pasta, meatballs, and taco meat in foil on site

TIP: Hummus, falafel, lentils, and daal can all be purchased in a powder form from the bulk aisle of many health food stores. Just add to boiled water and wait a few minutes. Eat with grilled pita.

YOUR CAMP KITCHEN

Before you can think about chowing down, you have to spend some time setting up shop. To do this safely and responsibly, you have a few options. If you are camping at an established site, use preexisting fire rings or areas designated for cooking to minimize your impact on your tasty outdoor surroundings.

The ideal situation is to use a camp stove instead of building a fire. Fires are outlawed in many states and regions so check with the area and make sure it's legal. Leave the infractions to parking tickets back in civilization. If you are able to build a campfire, use downed wood, such as loose twigs and branches. Never break off branches or strip a tree in any way. That's just bad karma, baby.

The Camp Stove

There are a lot of inexpensive and deluxe camp stoves on the market. Resist the urge to buy the cutest model: think about what kinds of meals you want to cook up, and for how many. If you are camping with your entire entourage or plan to fix Thanksgiving dinner, you may want to bring something with dual burners. Just a thought. If you are hiking deep into the woods, bring along a lightweight, easy-to-use model (some even fit in your pocket, although they may leave an unsightly bulge). Some are collapsible, and some can be unhooked from their fuel source or broken down for easier portability. If you mostly car camp or work out of a fifth-wheel camper, you can invest in a bigger, sturdier stove.

When it comes to powering it up, there are butane- or propane-fueled stoves. The canisters are heavier and non-recyclable, but the fuel works great in warm and moderate conditions. Kerosene is a dirtier choice but it's cheap and can be found everywhere. White gas is inexpensive, performs well in all conditions, and is easily found in the United States. Both kerosene and white gas require more prep than butane and propane. Denatured alcohol is renewable and provides quiet cooking, but its heat output is lower so cooking takes longer. Like kerosene, unleaded gas is messy and can clog the stove. It's cheap, but who cares when you are stuck with soot in your hair?

As a Betty, you may want to consider how this bad boy performs before purchasing. Most stoves will display facts such as the average boiling time and how long the stove will burn before the fuel needs to be replaced.

Think in terms of energy conservation. Use a lid when cooking, don't boil water if you don't have to, that sort of thing. You don't want to run out of fuel before you cook your fourth bratwurst. That would be tragic.

Light My Fire

If you are permitted to build a fire in your campsite, you may want to opt for the open flame over a camp stove. There are still guidelines for cooking with fire in the forest.

Build your fire in a pre-existing fire ring to contain the impact (see page 82). If you are in a pristine location but you don't opt use use a camp stove, lessen the impact of your presence by using a fire pan or building a fire mound. Fire pans are flame-resistant metal trays with sides high enough to contain wood and ashes. A mound is created by laying a tarp down on your cooking site and placing a round mound of mineral soil, six to eight inches thick with a flat top. For pan and mound fires, keep the fire small. And when cooled, scatter the ashes away from the campsite and return the soil to its original location.

Limit your cooking to a surface that will withstand your activities, such as a rock outcropping or vegetation-free soil. Ideally, it should be 200 feet from your tent and any natural water source. If you can determine which way the wind is blowing, scout out a location downwind from camp.

Avoid dropping food on the ground or feeding wildlife (all vittles should be going straight into your mouth!) and just like your other, uh, waste, pack out any food leftovers or trash.

Your Backcountry Gourmet Gear

The bare bones list of your kitchen essentials:

- ✧ Camp stove and fuel
- ✧ Cooler
- ✧ Skillet
- ✧ Saucepan with lid
- ✧ Large mixing spoon
- ✧ Plates
- ✧ Sharp knife
- ✧ Forks, knives, and spoons for each person
- ✧ Ziploc (to shake and bake and to secure your aromatic foods)
- ✧ Thermos (for mixing up liquids)

TIP: When not in use, hang your foodstuffs (see page 75). When preparing your meals cover foods with a light cloth and place out of the sun to keep them as cool as possible.

KEEP YOUR COOL

Coolers have come a long way, Betty. They can keep ice for days, not to mention your other beverages and foodstuffs.

If you are car camping, consider keeping your airtight cooler in the car to further protect it from critter invasion. Even better, there are large electric coolers that plug into your car's lighter socket. As for traditional coolers, look for one with wheels, tight-fitting lids, drain plugs, and recessed handles (the cooler can double as a table or bar). It should be sturdy and built to last. Some coolers can keep ice and items cold up to six days in temperatures as high as 90 degrees. Adding cold packs and blocks to your cooler can also help keep your larder cool. What could be better than an icy margarita after a long day of bird-watching in 90-degree weather? Um, nothing.

If you are backpacking, you can strap on portable insulated coolers that can hold up to a twelve-pack and foodstuffs as well. The refrigeration is not as effective, but they have removable liners and can fold flat when not in use. Cold packs are necessary for these coolers.

TIP: Leave easily bruisable foods at home, as well as food that provides very little nutritional value, such as mushrooms. Use your space for foods that will give you the biggest bang for the buck.

LIQUID ASSETS

Staying hydrated in the outback is a bit more challenging than simply downing Evian on the treadmill. You have to mete out your water, and it's difficult to carry a variety of foods and beverages that will properly hydrate you. To that end, add some zip to your basic water by mixing some H_2O with a Crystal Light packet (now available in individual portions) or an Emergen-C powder (for both flavor and

vitamins). Some tea companies make cold-brewed packets that allow you to brew tea without hot water. Even adding just a wedge of lemon or lime to your canteen can add a bit of flavor and variety to your drink, not to mention a shot of vitamin C. Remember: No one likes scurvy.

If you are able to bring some bevvies in addition to water (that is, you persuaded your hunky companion to portage extra drinks), pack a few individual juice boxes (they are great mixers for certain hard liquors like vodka, which you may have also found room for in your gear). To keep your drinks cool, tie your bottles or cans in a stuff sack and tie it up with webbing or a secure rope to a rock or tree and put it in the river. It will stay in the cold part of the river without floating away, gravitating toward the moving water. You can freeze any non-carbonated beverages before you go so they can thaw out slowly while hiking, and they'll be cool when you're ready to quench your thirst. For more ideas about libations, check out chapter 5, page 96.

DINING ALFRESCO

Now that your kitchen has been set up and your food secured, you can turn your attentions toward the much more pleasurable task of cooking and eating.

KITCHEN AIDS: A FEW TIPS

THE FIVE-SECOND RULE: If you drop any food on the ground, no worries. The five-second rule doesn't apply in the wild. If you can wipe or rinse off most of the dirt, it doesn't smell, and the color looks sort of normal, give it a go. Remember to breathe through your nose, and if you have to, close your eyes. If you just can't stomach the dirty food, pack it away to dispose of later. Leaving it on the ground will attract attention, and not the good kind.

FOOD IS FUEL: Some foodstuffs or meals you whip up may not be up to your culinary standards, but you might need the sustenance to get you back to your favorite corner bistro. Actually, make a reservation for the day after you get back so you have motivation to power through your wilderness adventure. The thought of steak frites with a side of ibuprofen has motivated me more than once through a nasty trail full of switchbacks.

SAUCE IT UP: If you've got booze to spare, consider cooking with wine or liquor. Booze is great for seasoning a sauce or flavoring a protein.

Fondue Delight

● ● ● ● ● ●

One of the easiest treats to whip up on your camp stove has got to be fondue, either sweet or savory. Melting cheese or chocolate has long delighted many a camper, so get ready to chow down. Anything, even many bugs (think of the protein!), can be swallowed when covered in chocolate, or for that matter, cheese! Consider dried beef, a less than crisp vegetable, or an overly stale chunk of bread. Stick it on a toothpick, dip it in cheese, and it becomes the most elegant of finger foods.

You'll need a saucepan and a skewer (a small downed branch will do just dandy) for each person. For a classic take on a fondue recipe, grate Swiss and Raclette cheeses and put them in an airtight container. Bring along ½ cup kirsch (a cherry brandy) in another small container. Combine these at your campsite when you're ready to fondue.

Before you just decide to go all low budget and make a Velveeta fondue, consider this. Many hard cheeses (such as some Roqueforts and parmesans) don't require refrigeration. Before trekking out of town, check with your local cheese expert (even someone who works behind a specialty cheese counter at your local superstore or Whole Foods) about which cheeses will do well at room temperature. Avoid the orange brick if you can.

Cheese(s) of your choosing

Various bite-sized dippers, including baby carrots, celery sticks, bell peppers, Vidalia onions, sugar snap peas, edamame, green beans, smoked salmon, salami, bread chunks, crackers, various grilled meats

Place the cheese (and kirsch, if you brought some) in your saucepan and put over medium heat on your stove. Stir constantly as the cheese melts. When everything is thoroughly melted, remove it from the heat source and place on the ground or a safe surface. Skewer your dipper and coat it with savory cheesey goodness. Enjoy!

When you are ready for dessert, rinse out your saucepan (or lick it clean) and drop some chocolate (whatever kind you fancy) into it, stirring and slowly heating it over the stove just like you did with the cheese. Reuse your skewer, and this time, dip any and all of the following into your gooey delight:

- apple slices
- orange segments
- clementines
- pineapple chunks
- pitted cherries
- figs
- apricots
- dried fruit
- raisins
- graham crackers
- marshmallows
- bread chunks
- granola bars

• • • • • • • • • • • • • Your Portable Pantry • • • • • • • • • • • • • •

Foodstuff	What to do with it
Trail mix	melt chocolate over it and let harden into a sweet dessert
Dried meat/salami	wrap around apple slices
Fruit	schmear with cheese spread
Snack bars	crumble up and mix with dried fruit for makeshift granola
Chocolate	fondue anyone?
Potato or tortilla chips	pair with jar of salsa, dress a baked potato
Salsa	jazz up with diced tomatoes, mango, jalapeno; top a burger
Pickles	full of juice, pair with cured meat for a charcuterie plate
Lemons, limes	season your protein, zest up a drink, add to salsa or guacamole
Avocados	top a burger, mash into guacamole
Marshmallows	drop into hot chocolate, layer into s'mores, dip into chocolate fondue
Graham crackers	layer into s'mores, dip into chocolate fondue, use as a crust for a snack pack pudding pie
Potato	wrap in tinfoil and bake in your stove or coals of your campfire
Dried cherries or apricots	add to a cheese plate
Nuts	chop and put on chicken, burgers

continued on next page

Foodstuff	What to do with it
Dried sunflower seeds	add to salad
Peanut butter	use in chocolate fondue, on sandwiches, on graham crackers, as a fruit dipper
Cereal	crush and coat your protein with it, dip into fondue, mix with nuts for amped-up GORP
Soy milk	travels great and can go unrefrigerated as long as it's unopened, use on cereal
Powdered milk	just add water
Bisquik	pancakes, dumplings, biscuits
Smoked salmon	in omelettes, with cheese, for fondue dipping
Chicken stock	soup, stew base
Spam	fry it up, crumble on a baked potato, add to an omelet
Salt, pepper, favorite spice	zests up all sorts of snacks and meals

What to bring if you have refrigeration of any sort:

Eggs	omelettes, pancakes, biscuits, scrambled eggs
Meat	stew, burgers, hot dogs, breakfast sausage, bacon (precook the bacon)
Milk	cereal, various baked goods
Cream cheese	bagels, top celery, whip into a dip
Seafood	preshape crabcakes or salmon patties before you leave and throw them on the grill or stove

Niçoise Salad

· · · · · ·

This tasty salad brings a soupçon of France to the forest.

1 pound asparagus and/or green beans, blanched in advance

2 cans good quality tuna, packed in olive oil

4–8 hardboiled eggs, peeled in advance and halved on site

1 cup Niçoise olives

1 small shallot, thinly sliced in advance

Coarse sea salt, to taste

Coarsely cracked ground pepper to taste

Dressing: ¼ cup olive oil, 2 tablespoons red wine vinegar, 1 tablespoon of Dijon mustard, 1 chopped anchovy

BEFORE YOU LEAVE HOME: Dump asparagus or green beans into rapidly boiling water for 2 minutes and plunge them into an ice water bath to retain green color and crispness. They will keep for several days in your cooler.

Mix your ingredients on site. Shake your small container of dressing and lightly coat ingredients.

Serves 4

Options:

🍴 Precook ziti or penne pasta, and mix with salad

🍴 Serve salad on greens (you can use a salad mix, romaine, red leaf, or butter lettuce)

🍴 Add capers or chopped marinated artichoke

🍴 Slice a big crusty hard Italian baguette and put all ingredients of your Niçoise salad in it. Press and wrap in tinfoil before you leave. Let the flavors seep into the bread.

Savory Stew

Make this savory stew in advance and bring it along. Like you, it only gets better with age.

- 1 pound stew meat, cut into bite-sized pieces
- ½ cup all-purpose unbleached flour
- 1 tablespoon vegetable oil
- 3 carrots, diced
- 2 celery sticks, diced
- ½ onion, diced
- 2 tablespoons butter
- 1 cup red wine, such as Cabernet Sauvignon
- 2 cups beef stock
- 1 cup chicken stock
- Coarse sea salt, to taste
- Coarsely ground black pepper, to taste
- 3 cups of root vegetables, such as potatoes, carrots, turnips, and parsnips, cut into ½-inch chunks

Place flour on a dinner plate and place a handful of meat on the plate at a time, coating each handful of meat with flour on all sides.

In a cast-iron skillet over low temperature, brown meat with 1 tablespoon vegetable oil until all sides are brown. Cover a plate with a paper towel. Remove meat from heat and place on the plate. Wipe out the pan with another paper towel.

In the same pan, sauté the carrot, onion, and celery (known as the *mirepoix*) in 2 tablespoons butter and soften until the onions and celery are translucent, about 5 minutes. Upon softening, pour in 1 cup of not completely dry red wine. Turn heat to high and boil until the pan is completely dry again.

Pour in 3 cups stock (2 cups beef, 1 cup chicken) and bring to a boil. Reduce heat and add meat to mixture. Taste for seasoning. Add your favorite root vegetables. Turn heat to low and reduce to stew consistency (as thick as you fancy, anywhere from 20 minutes to 1 hour).

Let cool completely to room temperature. Transfer to an airtight container and refrigerate. When you are ready to reheat, transfer your stew to a saucepan and reheat to your satisfaction.

Serve with a small baguette. Slice it almost all the way through, add a thin pat of butter between each slice, wrap in tinfoil, heat, and serve with stew.

Serves 4

Cheese Dip
• • • • • •

If you fancy Velveeta, this classic also repurposes the orange brick in the most delightful of ways. Melted and mixed with salsa, you have a cheese dip that satisfies the most serious junk food jones.

1 pound Velveeta
1 cup salsa
Tortilla chips

Heat the Velveeta over medium heat, stirring constantly. You may not be able to control your heat so just do the best you can and watch your pot so that it never boils. Stir in the salsa until thoroughly blended, remove from heat, and dip your chips into it. Yum. How easy was that?

Easy Peasy Pasta Salad

• • • • • •

Pasta salad keeps quite well at room (or ambient) temperature. Here, the dressing acts as a preservative of sorts as it infuses the pasta and vegetables with flavor. To be safe, do not add cheese, or only add it when you are ready to sit down and carbo load.

1 12-ounce box of rotelle pasta, cooked until slightly al dente and drained

1 green bell pepper, chopped into ½-inch chunks

1 red or yellow bell pepper, chopped into ½-inch chunks

1 red onion, chopped into ½-inch chunks

1 medium-sized zucchini, chopped into ½-inch chunks

2 carrots, diced

1 6-ounce jar of marinated artichokes, diced

⅓ cup Kraft Zesty Italian salad dressing

Salt and pepper, to taste

BEFORE YOU LEAVE HOME: Toss all of your ingredients together, adding dressing until the ingredients are thoroughly coated. Seal in an airtight container and keep sealed until you are ready to chow. At the campsite: Shake the container before opening and enjoy. For a little protein, mix in a can of chicken or tuna.

Serves 4

BEYOND THE BASICS

Even if you are cooking dogs and burgers, there's no reason to just slather them in ketchup and yellow mustard. Zest up brats, hot dogs, and hamburgers by using the following (prepping in advance, of course):

- Sauerkraut
- Dijon mustard mixed with a small dollop of olive oil and tarragon
- Caramelized onions
- Ketchup punched up with any of the following: roasted garlic, mayonnaise, chives, Tabasco, chili pepper flakes, roasted red pepper, chipotle soaked in water and thrown in the blender, Asian Sriracha hot sauce

SIMPLE SNACKING

Take some snack and comfort food classics on the road:

S'mores: *The* camp classic. Layer chocolate and toasted marshmallow between graham crackers.

Ants on a Log: Spread peanut butter on celery and top with raisins.

PB&J: Make peanut butter and jelly sandwiches, or even layer the two spreads on crackers.

Snack packs: Whether it's pudding, applesauce, or pull-tabbed chicken and tuna cans, just open the container and get to it.

Crostini: Before you go, grill slices of a crusty bread with a bit of olive oil. On site, warm in foil and make a tasty crostini by topping with an Italian salsa of diced tomatoes, olive oil, garlic, balsamic, and basil (you can make this before you leave as well). You can also buy a jar of tapenade and spread it over your bread.

Pancakes: What's not to like? Just don't try to harvest your own syrup from that sticky maple trunk. It doesn't exactly work that way. You can find mixes that just require water and with a skillet and camp stove, you've got a great breakfast, lunch, or dinner treat.

Baked potatoes: Wrap in tinfoil, lay on hot coals, and cook for

20 minutes or so, making sure you turn them every so often.

Grilled cheese: With a bit of butter-flavored spray, grill up some cheese sandwiches in a skillet.

Jiffy Pop popcorn: With its self-contained popping pan, all you have to do is put it over your heat source, shake it, and wait for the kernels to pop.

Chili: Spruce up canned chili with a few spices (that you so cleverly mixed up in a baggie before you left your cushy pad) and fresh ingredients (onions, garlic, and jalapenos, which can also be used for salsa or burger embellishment).

Roast a head of garlic: Drench in olive oil, wrap securely in heavy-duty foil, and pop over the fire.

. . . .

TIP: As you head to the trail, keep an eye peeled for produce stands. You can get amazing seasonal fruits and vegetables that can often be eaten raw or with minimal preparation. And stopping to chat with locals is another way to add to your Betty adventure.

PACKET DISHES

Called *en papillote* in fine cuisine, it literally means cooking in paper. In your camp kitchen, however, you will be cooking an entire meal in heavy-duty aluminum foil (don't use flimsy foil or it will burn and stick to your dish) over your fire or stove.

While there are a few delicious recipes to start with here, there are unlimited ways to cook this way. Use your imagination and some of your favorite ingredients to make your own signature dish.

PROPER FOLDING TECHNIQUE FOR YOUR PACKET: Take a generous piece of foil and mark it in thirds in one direction. Draw the two edges up, leaving the third middle panel as the bottom of your packet. Making a triangle, hold the two edges together and roll them down to secure the top. Now roll up each side in the same way, securely crimping all edges to keep liquid and ingredients intact.

When it's time to cook your packet, place it on the side of the fire, not directly over the hottest area. Err on the side of cooler temperatures and cook your packet longer.

NOTE: Coat the inside of the foil in oil; otherwise, the food will adhere to it.

Souvlaki

• • • • • •

Here's a rustic take on a Greek favorite.

The skewers should be made in advance. You'll need:

- 1 pound ground lamb
- 2 slices of sandwich bread, pulsed in food processor and ground to crumbs
- 1 egg
- 2 cloves garlic, minced
- Pinch of salt
- Pinch of coarse ground pepper

Mix meat, bread, egg, garlic, salt, and pepper like you are making meat loaf. Take a skewer and form the mixture on the skewer. Lay in a flat airtight plastic container and keep in a coolor until ready to cook. If you like, you can also form the meat into balls and place in a Ziploc bag instead.

Parcook rice in advance as well, cooking with chicken stock instead of water. Add a pinch of saffron or turmeric. Cook rice until al dente: it should be almost done, with the outer part cooked and the inner rice still hard. Pack in a separate airtight container.

On site, assemble the packets.
For each packet, add:

- 2 skewers
- 1 cup rice, parcooked
- 1 tablespoon dried oregano
- 3–5 cherry tomatoes
- 3 tablespoons red wine vinaigrette (see page 54)

Place over a low to medium heat source. Check packet after 20 minutes. Serve with charred pita bread (throw onto a skillet or grill with or without a smidge of olive oil to char slightly) and a dollop of whole-milk yogurt (or sour cream).

Serves 4

Rockin' Moroccan Tagine
• • • • • •

Impress your campanions with this exotic and easy vegetarian dish. The great thing about this is that not much needs to be sliced, diced, or prepped in advance.

Add the following to each packet (one for each person):

- ½ cup dried couscous
- 1 cup vegetable broth
- ½ cup canned garbanzo beans (or, ¼ of a 14-ounce can)
- ¼ yellow onion, sliced in advance

Handful of golden raisins
2 tablespoons pine nuts or almonds
Pinch of nutmeg
Coarse sea salt, to taste (add somewhat liberally since the
    couscous will absorb a lot of the flavor)
Coarse ground pepper, to taste
Juice of ¼ lemon, cut in advance

Add ingredients into packet, wrap securely, and cook over fairly direct heat, 10 to 12 minutes. If you are cooking over a fire, place a large rock on the slope of the mound or fire pit and place the packet on the stone to cook.

BAGS OF FOOD

Yes, you also have the option of bringing along a few bags of freeze-dried entrees, such as beef stroganoff, paella, and even Thai dishes. Perfectly edible and full of needed nutrients, they are highly portable and just require boiling water (many cook right in the pouch!). If you are camping for several days or longer, consider bringing along a few of these packets and zesting them up with some fresh vegetables and spices. Cook them up in the pouch, pour them into a saucepan or skillet, and add some chopped onions, peppers, chili powder, whatever.

TIP: Never feed the wildlife, no matter how cute the Trickster McBandit raccoon. You can upset the ecosystem and attract unwanted critters to your campsite.

IF YOUR FREEZE-DRIED FOOD IS:	ADD:
Mexican, Southwestern dishes	Velveeta, chili powder, cumin, pepper, onions, green peppers; top with guacamole, salsa
Pasta, Italian	black pepper, oregano, fresh basil, garlic, onion, olive oil; top with grated parmesan
Stew	Chopped vegetables, canned corn, chili powder; top with cheese, crumbled tortilla chips, dumplings, chunks of bread
Thai	chopped peanuts, curry powder, fresh basil, chili pepper, garlic, ginger, coriander, cumin, cilantro, star anise, cinnamon
Japanese	ginger, tofu, wasabi, cucumber, daikon radish, water chestnuts
Indian	curry powder, cumin, cilantro, fennel, turmeric, coriander, fenugreek
German	sauerkraut, gherkins, chopped sausage, beer
Spanish	saffron, cumin, rice, white wine
Greek	olives, oregano, lemon, garlic, olive oil, rice; top with crumbled feta

PROTECTING YOUR PANTRY

You went to a lot of trouble to lug your larder to your campsite (or you took considerable effort persuading your companions to do it all for you). So the last thing you want is for critters large or small to ferret out your fondue fixings. If you aren't chowing down, you really must tie up your food. There's no way around it.

Find a good location about 100 feet from your campsite, perhaps adjoining your camp kitchen for easy access. Secure all your food in Ziploc bags or containers with airtight lids. Using nylon rope and a sturdy bag, rig up a food bag 10 feet high and 4 feet from the tree trunks. This is your best chance to prevent bears, let alone any smaller animals, from filching your niblets. Hang your trash along with your food.

For added security, consider bringing along a canister specially designed to keep out bears. It holds a good amount of food, has locks that we can work but that bears can't, is smooth and round so bears can't grip onto it, and is made of extremely durable, lightweight material.

If you are not in bear country, just place your food and waste in separate bags and tie them to a rope. Sling the bags and rope over a branch when you don't need to feed.

CLEANING UP WHEN CLEARING OUT

Rinse your cooking gear with portaged water. Some might say to drink the dirty water as it will help with hydration and leave no trace, but I don't have the stomach for it. If you do, you get the Backcountry Betty Medal of Honor.

And when you vacate the premises, leave things as pristine as possible. Replace any soil you disturbed and fluff tamped down grass, clean out the fire ring, scatter ashes, pick up and pack out your trash. Spread any excess wood around the wilderness area, place used rocks black side down. To go the extra mile, use a downed branch to sweep away your footprints as you leave. This has the added benefit of throwing anyone hunting you down off your trail.

Chapter 4

......

CAMPING IT UP

Oh, camp. Visions of toasted marshmallows, pine-fresh scents (that aren't coming from an air freshener dangling from your rearview mirror), and campfire ghost stories dance in your head. And then you reach the clearing.

There's nothing there, not even a fire pit. No running water, no babbling brook. And there's certainly nothing resembling that decadent love tent you remember seeing the bad guy enjoying in *Raiders of the Lost Ark*. How the heck are you supposed to make s'mores when there's nothing in place for your campstravaganza? Where is the outdoor shower and the sumptuous down-filled tent?

In your dreams, that's where. But there are some measures you can take to Betty things up. "Roughing it" doesn't have to translate into "foregoing all traces of comfort and style." In fact, you—a camping novice in some respects—can teach the most seasoned and grizzled of outdoorsmen and women a thing or two.

Repeat after me: Practicality and comfort are not mutually exclusive. Say it, memorize it, and then drill the idea into your campanions. When your best friend tries to talk you out of setting the table for dinner, tell her to go make up the guest tent. When your boy tells you that it's just a waste of time to set up cairns around the perimeter, send him off to check on the camp stove (remember to put the rocks back where you found them when you leave). As we've learned from *The Secret* and good, old common sense, there's little to be gained from negative thinking. In a bad frame of mind, however are you going to meditate effectively in your Zen dirt garden, let alone pitch your "decatent"?

Regardless of whether you are able to turn your campsite into something Martha Stewart would call a "good thing," you can still roast marshmallows, tell ghost stories, and tuck into a snug bed roll. All of your exertions and exterior decorating should be done with the idea of creating an unforgettable (in a good way) camping experience that you will be eager to repeat (after the pain in your quadriceps subsides and you've taken a three-day shower, of course).

Because, after all, practicality and comfort are not mutually exclusive. And a Betty brings the two together beautifully in the backcountry.

SETTING UP CAMP

First things first, pick a suitable location to make camp. If you are near water, it's logical to set up shop nearby. Not only will the water be handy for rinsing off or frolicking, its soothing sounds will help lull you to sleep and mask the other, more alarming sounds of the wilderness. However, wilderness guidelines urge you to locate your campsite well away (at least 200 feet) from any water source.

If you are camping amongst others, pitch your tent near the hunkiest group of mountain men you can find. Better yet, let them pitch it for you. You know you're helpless like a fox, so use those wily skills to your advantage.

Look for level ground in a clearing away from low-hanging trees, bushes, and flora. You'll need to clear the area of brush (remove downed branches, leaves, and loose debris, making sure to return it to its original condition before you leave) before you can start a campfire (which is often illegal, so check your local and state laws). Use preexisting sites to minimize the impact on your surroundings. If no existing campsite is available, look for an area of soil or rocks to make camp, rather than a grassy field or heavily foraged area that will feel the effects (even if they are minor, in your opinion) of your sojourn. If it's already done for you, you'll save a lot of time, time that can be better spent mixing up camp cocktails.

Speaking of cocktails, if you plan on raising a ruckus, it's only right that you scout out a location far away from the maddening crowds (i.e., anyone inclined to be irked by your shenanigans). It's crazy, I know, but some people actually like peace, quiet, and communing with nature. Go figure.

Tents at a Glance

Three-season tents: Intended for spring, summer, and autumn trips in moderate climates. They can withstand wind and rain but don't expect to weather a massive snowstorm comfortably.

Four-season tents: Fine to use during warmer months, but these rounded tents are built for serious weather and have additional or heavier poles and sturdier canopies (side walls).

Convertible tents: These tents go both ways: four-season tents that can be stripped of some poles and have zippered panels that can be opened during temperate weather.

Warm-weather tents: As you'd expect, they are lightweight and feature mesh walls for maximum ventilation.

Bivy sacks: Single-person shelters. Nothing more needs to be said about these, since you don't plan on sleeping solo.

Family tents: These are challenging to carry into the backcountry, unless your group is willing to divvy up the tent components. These roomy tents are ideal for slumber parties, although you still might lack the headroom for a proper pillow fight.

RAISING THE ROOF

Pitching a tent is not usually a piece of cake, although tents and camping gear have gotten much, much easier to assemble and use.

Before you pitch your tent, you have to choose one. Take into

consideration the season and conditions in which you are camping. If you are camping in the winter (why, I don't know), go for a heavier, four-season tent. Convertible tents offer you the flexibility of changing size and ventilation. Two-person tents sound über-cozy, but for two adults who might have gear, not to mention a desire to knock hiking boots, the quarters might prove a little bit too close.

Before pitching your tent, lay a tarp on the ground. If it rains on your wilderness parade, water will build up outside your tent and roll under the tarp, not your camping crib. It should be slightly smaller than your tent (otherwise, water will sit on the tarp).

If you don't have to carry your gear too far and your tent is roomy, consider busting out a battery-powered air mattress. You'll be elevated from the hard ground. Bring real bedding and lay a comforter or thick pad on the mattress, so that you have a warm layer between you and the cold air of the mattress and the ground.

TIP: Make sure you measure your bodies (both width and girth) and bedding before selecting a tent to make sure it will be comfortable and accommodating.

The Guest Room

Did you go off and invite others to join you on your trip who don't quite have your Betty willingness to rock the wilderness? Is she expecting crepes for breakfast alfresco? Is he looking forward to a hot shower under the wide open sky? Well, they are going to be disappointed no matter what, but you can ease the pain by infusing the campsite and their "guest room" with some flair. Sneak into his or her tent and place some tiny travel-sized toiletries, a small book by Jack London or John Muir, or even a package of homemade trail mix. The thoughtfulness will lessen the pain of going without a bathroom, let alone a bathroom with heated floor tiles.

BURN, BETTY, BURN!

This is why you trekked for what seems like days. You wanted to sit around a campfire, warming yourself and passing around the flask. You'll get your wish, but you need to create a safe and comforting campfire before you can feel the heat. But a word of caution: many states have outlawed campfires in wilderness areas, so check local regulations (and take the weather into consideration) before firing up. They can cause wildfires, damage the soil, or consume wood that is better left where it is.

Opt for a campsite with a preexisting fire pit or fire ring, if it's available. If you haven't selected a site with a fire pit, you'll need to build a fire mound or use a fire pan. Scout out a dry clearing sheltered from the wind, at least six feet away from low branches, brush, and, duh, your tent or cabin. Look for an area replete with downed wood and if the site has been used as a camp before, set up your fire on the spot that's been previously used for a campfire.

The Mound Fire

With a spade or shovel (if you didn't pack such a tool in that backpack you bought because it made your butt look good, do the best you can with any branch you see lying around or any other equipment you brought with you), fill a large sack with mineral soil (replace it when you are done). Lay out a tarp or plastic trash bag on the ground. Clear the area around the tarp, gathering any sticks, leaves, dry brush, needles, and the like. Pile the debris away from the pit; it will make perfect tinder and kindling for your fire. Dump the soil on the tarp, forming it into a flat-topped mound that's about six or eight inches high. It should have a circumference wider than the height. Keep the fire small—use small pieces of downed wood. When the fire is completely out, scatter the ashes over a wide area and return the mineral soil to it original location.

The Pan Fire

Fire pans are flame-resistant metal trays with sides high enough to contain wood and ashes (usually three-inch lips). While there are portable, lightweight pans you can purchase, you can improvise with household items such as a metal garbage can lid. Clear the area around the pan and then prop it up on a few rocks to protect the ground. Layer the bottom of the pan with sand, add tinder and kindling, and light up. Like a mound fire, scatter the cold ashes away from the campsite.

At this point, you should feel pretty proud of yourself and take a break to have a snacklet or bevvie. You've already gathered some tinder and kindling to start your pan or mound fire, but when you're feeling refreshed, look for downed logs, bark, and dead wood that can serve as firewood. Respect your environment; do not cut branches or wood from any live trees or flora.

TIP: Carry matches, lighter, or other firestarter in a waterproof bag.

FIRESTARTER/AID	TINDER	KINDLING	FIREWOOD
petroleum jelly	pine needles	twisted tissue	dry logs
lipstick	twigs	small sticks	large branches
hand sanitizer	bark	larger twigs	
perfume	wood shavings	pinecones	
matches	dry brush		
lighter			

BUILDING A FIRE

If you do have a designed campfire area and campfires are legal in your neck of the woods, it's time to lay your fire. S'mores are in your near future! You can lay a fire in a variety of ways—heck, you can even create a woody sculpture or design—but there are certain guidelines you need to follow if you want to have a crackling, safe fire in no time.

Create a pile of tinder in the center of your fire pit. Angle the kindling against the side of the tinder pile, creating a lean-to. You can also build a teepee of kindling, angling twigs so that they meet at a peak over the tinder. Leave plenty of room between the kindling and the tinder so that air can ventilate.

Before you light up, fill two buckets (or some sort of receptacle) with water or sand and place them near the pit. Safety first!

Okay, here we go. Grab your match or lighter and, standing out of the wind or cupping your hand, carefully light up and ignite the edges of the tinder. Blow gently on the flame. As the fire catches, add small twigs and branches. Once the fire is going, gradually add larger wood (throwing too many logs on too fast can smother your efforts). Stoke it whenever the fire starts to get low. When you do throw another small log on the fire, don't *throw* it. Just place it carefully, to avoid flying sparks and embers. At this point, you are probably in heaven sitting around the fire, telling your favorite joke, and sipping your favorite drink. To really send yourself to the moon, throw a pinecone or two onto the blaze. Sharp pine scents are a fragrant pick-me-up.

When the fire burns out, douse the embers with water or sand. When it stops steaming and hissing, scatter the ashes and return the mound soil to where you found it and you're safe to go.

AMBIANCE

A snug tent and a crackling fire go a long way to heating up your campsite, but as a Betty, your work is far from done. There is still much to be done to achieve the kind of sexy campsite worthy of you.

First, let's focus on your love nest, that is, your tent. So you've got the tent up and your bedroll (or even air mattress, if you aren't far from your car) up and running. The basics are there, so what's a Betty to do next? If car camping (i.e., camping a short distance from your ride), using your old bed linens is a yummy, easy way to add additional comfort to your tent. They don't add a lot of weight to your gear, and bring civility and a touch of home to your unfamiliar surroundings.

To sex up your bunk, consider draping exotic fabrics (which can double as a sarong) on your bed or from the ceiling. Secure it in the center of the tent and gently drape it and pin it to the sides for a billowing "sultan in a sandstorm" effect. If the weather is agreeable, keep as much of your gear and equipment outside your tent so you can focus on sleep and other horizontal activities in your sex chamber.

When it comes to lighting, let me just say that candles + tents =

disaster. Instead, hang or place camping lanterns or flashlights safely away from fabric and on the lowest setting. Affix acetate or clear plastic stickers to your lantern so that it emits a soft or patterned glow. Turn them off as soon as possible and feel your way in the darkness. And remember to pack extra batteries (rechargeable batteries don't do you much good without an outlet to plug into).

How Illuminating

A few stylish and practical options to lighting up the scene:

✧ Glow sticks

✧ Lanterns: butane, electric, liquid fuel, candle

✧ Camp stove

✧ Fireflies

✧ Moon and the stars

If you do choose to bring along a candle lantern, keep it well away from your bedding, sleeping bag, and tent canopy. But there are butane, electric, and liquid fuel lanterns that are effective alternatives to candles. Let the only fire burning in your tent be of the metaphorical kind.

Scent is important and the natural smell of the wilderness is one of the world's free gifts. With that in mind, amp up your tent with lavender and rosemary pillows or sachets (this will also help to mask any lingering hygiene issues).

While you want to be warm and cozy in your tent, you must also ventilate. If it's too cold to unzip the tent or open up a mesh panel or window, you must have a tent made out of a breathable fabric. If not, moisture will condense inside the tent, creating a damp, clammy environment—not exactly comfortable.

To soften things up, fill a bag with sand for an ingenious beanbag seat, cushion, or eye pillow. You can also fill a bag with dirty laundry and use that as a cushion as well. Make it keep working for you, even if you can't stand the sight or smell of it one minute longer. Just keep looking around you for items you packed in or loose and downed materials in the wild that you can use to make your campsite both eye-catching and comfy.

LANDSCAPING YOUR CAMPSITE

When beautifying your camp, you don't need to clip the shrubs into topiaries of shoes and lipstick tubes (although I'd like to see it). Rather, there are ways to "Bettify" the area with found objects and things you have on your person.

"She's like the wind through my tree." Give new meaning to Patrick Swayze's lyrics by creating some natural wind chimes. Tie some loose twigs or bark to some branches or vines. If you have twine handy, even better. Poke a hole in the bark or wrap the twine around an offshoot of the branch and tie them close together from a sturdy branch.

If you are near a sandy area, or even a dry patch of dirt, create a Zen garden. Artfully place several large rocks within the area and then, with a loose branch, driftwood, or walking stick, swirl designs into the ground. Find a comfortable space on the ground and meditate on your garden until you feel peaceful or hungry. To erase your work and start over, use a dirty t-shirt or a downed leafy branch to wipe the area clean.

Cairns are piles of rocks used as small altars or markers along a trail or in the wilderness. Line the path to your campsite or ring your tent with stacked rocks from your surroundings. You can also use rocks to create crude outlines of your favorite things: a bird, leaf, martini glass, whatever you fancy. When you break down your campsite, return the rocks to their original locations.

If you are surrounded by vines, braid downed vines together and decorate a pine tree with your garlands.

Color Guard

Gardeners and bird-watchers know what colors will attract and repel birds and wildlife. But it's not only flowers and foliage that draw a critter's attention. I was once sitting outside in a red bathrobe when a hummingbird zoomed right up and stared me down, as if to say, "You're not a flower." Of course, I smell like a bouquet of flowers, which only added to its confusion. Poor thing. Anyway, here are a few colors that will draw the eye of various winged creatures.

Red	hummingbirds
Pink, fuchsia	hummingbirds
Orange	butterflies
Purple	butterflies
White	moths
Dark blue, black	biting flies

And be aware when setting up camp that the following trees are popular amongst forest creatures for their shelter and/or food possibilities. So you might want to avoid making camp in a stand of madrona trees; otherwise you might get a raccoon or two sauntering up around dinner time looking for a snack.

◇ Crabapple
◇ Cypress
◇ Madrona
◇ Oak, various
◇ Pecan
◇ Persimmon
◇ Red maple

THE TRASH PLAN

Not the sexiest of topics, but a necessary one. It's a whole lot sexier to plan this in advance than to have to deal with it on the fly. If you didn't bring along a bearproof container and you are in the back-country (which, as a Backcountry Betty, you probably are), you'll have to secure your trash and your food by hanging it.

Scout out a location at least 100 feet from your campsite. With a long length of nylon rope (30 to 100 feet long), tie up your food in a sturdy bag and your trash in another. If the area you are in is not known for bear raids on your "pickanick basket," just sling the bag of food over a high tree branch. However, if there is danger of your pantry being pilfered, you'll have to string up your food and waste at least 10 feet above the ground and 4 feet from the tree trunks; this is your best chance of keeping paws off your stuff.

Chapter 5
......

ENTERTAINING AT
CAMP BETTY

C re you wrecked from hiking since dawn through miles and miles of wilderness to set up your camp? Or did it take you half an hour to set up camp because you are car camping at an established location with indoor plumbing? However you reached your final destination, you are most likely ready to relax, kick back, and enjoy the novelty of your location. In other words, you are ready to rock the wilderness, Betty-style. You've partied alfresco, sure, but it's usually on a friend's patio with a perfectly blended Manhattan in your manicured hand.

This is not exactly the same.

But that's not to say that you can't have an equally memorable and enjoyable time, even without the crystal double old-fashioned glasses.

With your campsite up and running, first take a breath and give yourself a well-deserved pat on the back. Better yet, ask someone to give you a massage. You have a sweet compound and are ready to bring on da action, bring on da funk. But having a killer campsite isn't the only thing required for a good time, although it's an excellent start.

You need to gather a posse (which won't be hard, since you attract people like bees to nectar), or at least a special honey to get your mountain mojo going. You'll then need to come up with some activities, snacks, and bevvies befitting the civilized and inventive hostess you are.

No sweat, right? Well, there are certain challenges even the best of Betties must take into account and overcome. You lack refrigeration, stemware, your favorite lighting concept, caterers, and confetti (resist the urge to blanket the pristine outdoors with that special chartreuse foil glitter you ordered for your last gala, even if it does sort of match the foliage in a weirdly unnatural way). But you have some things that are potentially much better, such as fresh piney air (no candle can do it justice, no matter how pricey and loaded with essential oils), gorgeous surroundings in earth tones that complement all skin tones, and your Betty ingenuity.

Assault his Senses

Make sure he's "camptivated" on every level.

Smell	A few drops of vanilla in a pot with water over your camp stove, grilled meat, pinecones
Sound	Singing, a portable stereo/iPod with playlists of camp-worthy seduction
Sight	A lacy tank (silk is a great choice) and snug shorts, the glow of the campfire, pedicured toes, a well-pitched tent, and a tidy campsite
Taste	Honey on lips for sweetness and softness, berries for slight stain and sweetness, something easy and sweet to eat (it all comes back to the fondue!)
Touch	Soft hair, silky skin, kissable lips; smooth fabrics (even the slippery feel of the bedroll can prove arousing)

GATHERING THE TROOPS

"If you pitch it, they will come."

The first element of a successful gathering is to, well, gather some lively folks. You can't send out a proper invitation or e-vite (chances are slim that you'll have WiFi in the woods), so what's a Betty to do? To reel in hunky mountain men and other Backcountry Betties, take some creative measures.

Wave an old blanket over your pan or mound fire to send up smoke signals. There is no standard language for smoke signals so just send up a few puffs and see who you reel in. Whether they are alarmed or intrigued, campers, hikers, and nature enthusiasts alike will head straight to your site to check out the action.

If a neighboring camper brought along his pup, attach an invite to the dog collar and send him back to his owner with a gentle pat on the behind. If you didn't bring along paper and pencil, sketch out your invite—you can even draw a treasure map, with X marking the spot of your camp—on downed bark with a pocket knife, berry juice, or lipstick. Invention is the mother of necessity, after all.

Resist the urge to set an actual mantrap. Digging a pit, hanging weighted nets from trees, and dangling a cold beer might prove effective, but it disturbs the wilderness and, let's face it, looks a little bit desperate, which you most certainly are not. Keep your efforts focused on finding willing participants, not prisoners (despite the delicious scenarios that conjures up).

Once you've added a few choice boys (and gals, if you're feeling generous and like spreading the wealth) to your camp posse, it's really time to impress.

Repurposing Your Outdoor Gear

Before you go moaning about how you have nothing cute to wear or decorate your campsite with, take a minute to think about what you *did* bring along and how you can multitask it.

Backpack	pillow, medicine ball
Sleeping pad	rug, yoga mat
Sleeping bag	log cushion, volleyball net
Water bottle	squirt gun, cocktail shaker
Tent	hammock, shower curtain

Cooler	coffee table, seat (make sure it's sturdy enough to hold your weight or you run the risk of harming the hinges), ottoman, clothes- or dishwasher
Walking stick	baton, shower curtain rod, Zen garden rake, limbo stick
Fleece jacket	oven mitt, camp flag or wind sock
Rain hats	water holder, bowl

Use found items to your stylish advantage (remember, don't remove or disturb anything if you can help it, keeping the "leave no trace" ethic in mind).

Pinecones	votive/taper holder
Pine needles	crush up and add to candle, bed padding, tie together for whisk broom
Fallen branches	hot dog/marshmallow stick, skewers, pole vault, limbo stick, backscratcher
Rocks/stones	hand warmers when heated next to stove, stack into cairns (return to original location when you leave), paperweights, hot stone massage, Mancala
Sand	foot exfoliant, ant farm, scrub out pots and pans (as long as you can rinse thoroughly), sandbags to weigh down tent or other items
Shells	individual appetizer bowls/cups, wind chimes, food covers
Seaweed	braid into necklace or crown, streamers, garlands, weave into placemats
Fallen leaves	placemats, coasters, hand fan

SETTING THE MOOD

Whether you're going for an elegant, mellow, or raucous feel to the festivities, you are the key to the party. Your mood will dictate the food, beverages, decorations, and yes, the other campers. While you can't go whole hog with themed napkins, insane party punches, and elaborately prepared hors d'oeuvres, you can employ your Betty wiles and trick out your campsite with items you packed in and found items.

SERVING IT UP

You've created a wilderness wonderland and drawn one or several party people to it. It would be nice if they all brought their own drinks and snacks but it's not likely, unless you requested that up front. No, it's up to you as the Bettiest hostess around to throw a party the likes of which the great outdoors has never seen. It'll be, well, *wild*.

At home, infuse your vodka with some fruit or berries two to five days before your trip. By the time you are ready to break ground, you'll have a flavored vodka that will need little to enhance it. To infuse, clean and squish two to four fistfuls of berries and drop them, along with a fifth of vodka, into an airtight, sealed container and let it be. You can also use other fruits. Just clean and slice one to three pieces and pop it in the container with the vodka.

Packing gear is always a challenge and when you need to have water in tow, alcohol can sort of fall by the wayside. But it doesn't have to. You can stow away a flask or two in your pack, and you can even take the bladder out of a box of wine (they've gotten better and better in recent years—really!) and let that fill up the nooks and crannies of your pack. If you do pack a flask or skin of some sort, consider bringing along dried packets of lemonade, Crystal Light, Tang, or Kool-Aid. Mix the powder with some water and add it to your hooch. Instant cocktail!

Crystal Light Mixology

Crystal Light comes in a variety of flavors these days. Pick your favorite liquor and pair it up with this handy, low-calorie drink mix (just add water). Suggestions are listed below.

Whiskey + Lemonade = whiskey sour

Vodka + Classic Orange = screwdriver

Rum + Strawberry = strawberry daiquiri

Peach Schnapps + Classic Orange = Fuzzy Navel

Rum + coconut milk + Pineapple Orange = Piña colada

Tequila + Raspberry Lemonade = Raspberry Margarita

If you don't want to pack a large amount of alcohol, consider stuffing a few airplane-sized bottles of booze into your gear. Or fill an empty water bottle with your favorite liquor; just be sure to label it. While you are always up for a nip, you probably won't be a happy camper if you grab a bottle for an ambitious day hike only to find thirst-quenching gin in it.

TIP: One 48-ounce Nalgene bottle holds about two bottles of wine. I'm just saying . . . (The company also makes 12-ounce flasks if your drinking preferences run more toward modest quantities.)

Being a Wild Child

Release your inner party animal, provided that you have someone along to keep an eye on you; that you aren't near a cliff, river, quicksand, or otherwise dangerous locale; and that the real animals (bears, snakes, raccoons, etc.) aren't going to come calling (check out what the indigenous wildlife is like before raising a ruckus). That said, being out of it out of doors has its perks: you probably won't care about going unwashed, you might get into the spirit of the whole "back to nature" nonsense your camping campanion keeps talking about, your downstairs neighbor won't call the police about the noise level, you won't wander into oncoming traffic, you don't have to worry about throwing up on something nice, waking up in a ditch is not necessarily a bad thing, etc.

FINGER FOODS

Aside from the tasty treats outlined in chapter 3, here are some snacklets that are easy to prepare and pass around your alfresco fiesta. Pass out moist towelettes first: everyone will appreciate your attention to detail and hygiene. Follow up by collecting the used wipes in a Ziploc bag.

- Strawberries
- Mini grilled cheese sandwiches and tuna melts

- Potato, tortilla, and bagel chips and dip
- Carrots and ranch dressing (it will travel well until you open it, so use it liberally once you break the seal)
- Salami and beef sticks
- Cocktail nut mix
- Chex Mix (whip up a batch before you leave home)

CAMPLIFY YOUR FUN

Sure, Betties embrace the classic camp activities, including telling ghost stories around the campfire, but why settle for that old "Girl with the Velvet Ribbon" story when you can shake and stir things up?

A Cappella Karaoke

If you think about it before you head to the hills, write the names of some popular (i.e., cheesy) songs on strips of paper. Then make campers draw a slip and—with feeling—sing it loud. Give a prize to the performer who really put his heart into it. Perhaps he butchered it but give him some props if he gave it all he had. Some song suggestions: ". . . Baby One More Time," "Bye Bye Bye," "The Greatest Love of All," "Livin' on a Prayer," "Sweet Home Alabama," you get the idea. If you don't have slips of paper handy, make things more interesting by having the group throw out song selections for the hapless crooner.

Charades

Charades are always a barrel of laughs. Again, if you are able to cut up strips with charade suggestions on them, so much the better. If not, challenge the campers to come up with their own words. But keep all charades related to the outdoors. It could be books *(Deliverance, Into Thin Air, Call of the Wild, Wilderness Tips)*, it could be film or television *(The Blair Witch Project, Lost, Friday the 13th, Little Darlings, Meatballs,*

Without a Paddle, Survivor, Point Break), it could be song ("Wild Thing," "Home on the Range," "On Top of Old Smokey"), it could be anything really, as long as it speaks to the surroundings.

Tall Tale or Ghost Story Roundtable

As a Betty, you certainly can bowl over an audience with your presence, wit, and command of language. But give others a chance to perform now and again. In fact, give them a showcase to unveil their talent for tall tales, their penchant for punchlines. Gather around the stove, warm your hands, and invite each person to tell their favorite bad joke, hilarious anecdote, or horrifying ghost story. Being a ham comes easy for some (i.e., you), but others might need the warmth of your campsite (and perhaps a toasty beverage) to loosen their tongues and their inhibitions.

To help others along, you can start a story and then ask each person around the circle to continue it. Start with "It was a dark and stormy night" and who knows where you'll end up. Depend-

ing on the imaginations of your friends, you might wind up at a rave party on a space station or spelunking in a cave in West Virginia.

Truth or Dare

Why do kids get to have all the naughty fun? Bring back this slumber party classic, but add some grownup questions and dares to the mix. Be as bawdy as a Betty is wont to be.

A few ideas to get the juices flowing:

TRUTHS

- Are you afraid of the dark?
- Tell us about your first kiss/sexual experience.
- Where do you see yourself in five years?
- What did you want to be when you grew up?
- Have you ever been attracted to someone much older or younger than yourself?

DARES

- Kiss the person to your left.
- Kiss the Betty.
- Howl at the moon.
- Yodel.
- Dance as if your life depended on it.
- Talk in a British accent for the rest of the evening.

Twilight Scavenger Hunt

While it's still light, give campers a list and charge them with heading out and looking for various flora and fauna. Instead of collecting the items, however, have them take pictures with their digital cameras (come on, most everyone has one these days). Give them a time limit and when you reassemble at camp, pass around the cameras to compare notes. Give a shout-out to the person who "collected" the most items on the list, as well as the camper who took the most stunning photo. When you are back in the land of USB ports, upload and share all of your photos for a lovely photo album of your adventure.

Cards

You can always play tried-and-true poker or blackjack, but it's a whole lot of fun to play rummy, canasta, hearts, or euchre (my Midwestern card game of choice). Bring enough decks of cards for your particular game. And don't expect others to know how to play. Print out rules before you leave and play a couple of practice hands until your friends get up to speed. It's probably a good idea to print out the order of winning hands in poker, too, if people are a bit rusty. You don't want things to get ugly when people start arguing over a flush and a straight. Regardless, you'll still take their money.

Mirror Image

Feeling cheesy? Well, channel your inner Marcel Marceau (a famous mime; actually, the *only* famous mime) and act out different actions, both classic and creative (trapped in a box, caught in a windstorm with an umbrella, trying on stilettos and admiring yourself in a mirror). If you really want to get silly, ask a friend to play the mirror game with you and mimic each other's motions as closely as possible. Again, mix it up. If you have a man following you, apply lipstick, put on pantyhose, play with your hair, and basically do anything you can think of that's super-girly. And then let him respond in kind, adjusting himself, chopping wood, lifting weights.

Stickionary

You don't have paper, pens, and easels, but you may have sand or large expanses of loose dirt. If this is the case, grab a downed branch and play some "stickionary." Divide into teams, and draw out puzzles for each other to guess. Keep track of the response time and the team with the lowest cumulative time wins. Some fun phrases, movies, books, or songs to try: *Wedding Crashers*, King of the Mountain, *Into Thin Air*, Bats in the Belfry, "Born in the U.S.A.," *Dead Men Don't Wear Plaid*, you get the idea.

Just Rewards

Everyone digs gifts, and how surprised will your friends be when you whip out a small party favor or prize? Some small but meaningful gifts to dole out and delight:

- ✧ small bottle of hand sanitizer
- ✧ wreath woven of found vines
- ✧ pinecone
- ✧ promise of a foot rub or sponge bath when you return to civilization
- ✧ compass
- ✧ water purification tablets
- ✧ energy bar
- ✧ water bottle
- ✧ moist towelette
- ✧ hiking socks
- ✧ pocket knife

Chapter 6
......

WILD THING, I THINK
I LOVE YOU

Y ou may think nothing sounds more *un*sexy than trying to maneuver in an un-air-conditioned tent while something vaguely
furry brushes up against your leg. Admittedly, there are a lot
of challenges to overcome when you are cavorting at your campsite
but there are also many, many delights to be found if you can open
yourself up to the fresh air, the skies filled with stars, the delicious
smell of loamy earth, not to mention your hunky mountain man . . .

Excuse me, I need a moment.

Whew, okay. What were we talking about?

As a Betty, you've undoubtedly dealt with the delicate issues of hygiene and, uh, elimination, but having sex can raise new concerns. Not
only do you have to worry about working your mojo in a small space, you
also have to think about how to clean up after getting, um, down.

But the important thing is to see the big picture here. You are
alone in the wild with each other, for goodness sakes! Take a moment to think about the advantages of your sexcape from the city:
no cell phone interruptions or work stress or car alarms blaring or
neighbors banging on the wall for you to keep it down or friends
pulling him away to get drunk at trivia night at the pub. Sounds
heavenly, doesn't it? Heaven with Handiwipes, of course, but a reli-
gious experience nevertheless.

So allow the brisk piney air, the twittering of birds, and the scenic
vistas to unleash your libido. After all, unless you're at a crowded
campsite, no one's going to hear you playing sleeping bag tag or
making sweet, sweet mountain music. This is the reason that you put
up with the hike and the ugly boots and the shorts that made your
thighs look like old forest tree trunks. And let's not even talk about
whatever slithered across the path an hour ago. Refocus. Think about
his rough fingertips trailing over your skin (may I suggest an erotic/
Swedish massage to work out the knots while working you into a

tizzy?). Can you hear the moans, cries, and screams of your unbridled passion? Imagine his strong arms (and, okay, legs) wrapped around you while the full moon shines down and an owl hoots somewhere over there.

Whew, okay, let's get to it.

WHEN IN ROME . . .

Or more appropriately, when in the wild, do as the wildlife would do. In other words, use the outdoors to your advantage. Even if you aren't camping or sleeping under the stars, vigorous exertion and fresh, crisp air can stir up your libido like nobody's business. Don't fight the feeling. Push him up against a tree (make sure there are no poisonous plants around) and have your way with him. Give him a bear hug as you follow him along a trail. While resting on a rock before resuming your trek, give him a sexy shoulder massage. While frolicking in the surf, throw him a come-hither look and let him do the rest. Let the fact that you're in the wild dictate more unrestrained behavior.

But—not to be contradictory—do it responsibly. That means not disturbing the actual wildlife or trampling down pristine areas while you are acting the tramp. Stick to preexisting campsites and, as your fingers do the walking, do your best to leave the untouched landscape untouched.

TIP: Set up your camp 200 feet (around 75 paces) from lakes, rivers, streams, and the like. While it may seem romantic to indulge in water play, it's not the approved environmental option. It's best to keep that at home in the comfort of your backyard bathtub.

TENT TACTICS

Tents are made to be snug and aerodynamic. In other words, there's not a lot of head space. I don't know who is designing them, but it certainly isn't what a randy girl like me would be sketching out. You will be positionally challenged. Count on it. Rather than trying to hunch over while on top, take the opportunity to explore some other positions and pursuits.

As far as straightforward sex goes, try lying side by side and working the angles. You might find a new favorite. Or you could just pitch a luxurious four-person tent and loll about. But you still might find that your shelter has low overhead. So if the conditions are favorable, you could unroll your sleeping bags outside and get busy. Just move back into the tent when it's time to rest and regroup.

If your sleeping bags are as compatible as you and your campanion, zip them together to create one large love cocoon. If not, just unzip your rolls and lay them out like blankets. Body warmth is always preferable over camping gear.

Indulge me with a little frank talk here. The wet spot blows, even in the comfort of your bed. There's no way around it . . . literally. You can imagine how less than ideal it is to encounter this in close quarters. Do yourself and your campanion a favor and use a condom. Yes, you may be in a loving, monogamous relationship and use another form of birth control but a condom is a tidy option while on a multiday trip away from faucets and pipes and showerheads. Toss the used condom into your waste bag to pack out with the rest of your trash. To further protect your linens and/or sleeping bag, lay down an old, clean towel or blanket that could suffer a bit of abuse. Remove it for sleeping, and pack it out with the rest of your dirty laundry at the end of the trip.

If you are engaged in other activities that might require cleanup but no condom, opt for the Wetnap and add it to your waste bag. It's as easy as that.

TIP: Many tents have a semi-translucent quality to the fabric, which can provide a bit of light or atmosphere to your goings-on. It's helpful when you want to see where you're going and what you're doing, without having to fire up a camping lantern. If you are finding it hard to see and feel your way in the dark, you can purchase glow sticks or even glow-in-the-dark zipper pulls that could be strategically placed in your tent for makeshift nightlights.

In Lieu of the Big Bang

- ✧ Make out for hours
- ✧ Scratch his forearms or buttocks lightly
- ✧ Look into each other's eyes
- ✧ Whisper delicious suggestions in his ear
- ✧ Nibble on his neck
- ✧ Suck on a finger or toe (please make sure you've cleaned up!)
- ✧ Massage his head
- ✧ Ask him questions about his sexual preferences, and then practice them
- ✧ Use your tongue (and your imagination)

DIAL DOWN THE VOLUME

Just like you want to avoid any physical impact on your surroundings, so too should you keep mum . . . at least as best you can. Not only do you want to avoid scaring off wildlife both large and small, it's probably wise to keep it down so as not to alert your fellow campers to your goings-on. If you are near a raging river or enduring a thunderstorm, you might be able to get away with howling at the moon or at least making strange dolphin-like noises while you're getting busy. But chances are, any cries of passion will disturb the night silence. So when you want to scream, stuff your mouth with fleece or gently bite his shoulder. Don't worry; both will be relatively clean.

Soundproofing Your Tent

Foams and padding are a few things used to soundproof rooms. It will be difficult to completely muffle screams of delight in a tent, but you can take a few preventative measures. First, zip up and batten down all tarps and tent coverings; it should be snug and shut off from the outdoors. Then you can drape a blanket or hook up your fleece garments to the inside of the tent walls, further adding insulation and noise buffers.

Make keeping quiet into a delicious game. The first one to moan or make a noise in any way has to make breakfast over the camp stove or pack out the TP bag. Don't worry; if your campanion is making you moan, you're probably still winning even if you lose.

A ROCK OR A HARD PLACE

Let's face it. For all the pluses about getting your sex on in the Amazon, padding is not high on the list. It's probably safe to say that your bedroll or the ground or the beach or a field of clover is not going to provide as much comfort as the crazy-spendy mattress you bought with a fat tax return.

Rather than put your back out, enjoy the ride by thinking ahead. Lay out your fluffiest layers of fleece under your sheets or bedroll. Look for loamy earth to roll around on. Change up your positions. Try sitting, not laying, on the rock while getting to it. Try standing if your heights are compatible. You'll have to get out of your comfort zone to be anywhere approaching comfortable. And use your surroundings to your advantage. On the beach? Mold the sand to conform to your bodies. In the jungle? Find some downed vines and hitch up a swing or hammock. Just a thought.

Location, Location, Location

Avoid the following areas when feeling randy:

- ❖ Pristine areas
- ❖ Rocky roads
- ❖ Quicksand
- ❖ Cliffs and sharp drops
- ❖ Well-trafficked trails
- ❖ Fire ant hills
- ❖ Caves with animal droppings
- ❖ Areas with active volcanoes
- ❖ Areas with ongoing partying
- ❖ Beachfront affected by high tide
- ❖ Patches of three-leafed plants (they could be poison oak, ivy, or sumac)

IN THE COMPANY OF STRANGERS

Has the glorious mountain vista or warm cerulean waters made you positively uninhibited? Are you screaming with abandon? Not to put a damper on things, because your Bettiness is something to behold, but speaking of beholding, you might draw the attention of admirers and perverts (they aren't mutually exclusive). And if you are so caught up (or tied up, for that matter) in your activities, you might not hear the catcalls, whistles, or heavy breathing.

So unless you are a bit of an exhibitionist or a voyeur yourself, take evasive measures. First of all, case the joint, or in this case, fan out and check the perimeter. Make sure you're alone. An abandoned campsite might indicate that the campers will return at any moment. Fresh footprints indicate that your location gets some traffic. Paw prints along with the footprints suggest a dog is also on the loose or the leash. Large paw prints by themselves should alert you to a large critter in the vicinity.

Have a friend create a distraction over *there*. Push him up against the side of the tree that's hidden from the trail. Use that large rock outcropping to shield you from prying eyes while making out on the bluff. If possible, wear as little as possible. This allows for easy access and time efficiency. Keep your eyes open. It's titillating and allows you to scan the area with your peripheral vision at the same time. Use dawn, dusk, and sunset to further mask your maneuverings. If you work with your surroundings, your partner in crime, and your gear, chances are good that you can avoid detection when indulging your desires.

GREAT FIRST LINES

Much has been written about just how hard it is to write a great opening line in a novel. Create your own work of art by taking turns starting a story or scenario. Let your companion pick up the ball (or imaginary pen, as the case may be) and flesh out your premise. For instance, you say, "It was a dark and stormy night . . . " He continues, "and her skin was wet from being caught in the downpour. Her sensible fleece provides little comfort against the raging storm and she's eager to peel off her sodden garments for a warm, dry blanket. Or she's just eager to peel off her wet clothes and lay down in front of a fire to dry her damp, bare skin."

You get the idea. Boy, do you ever.

A few other "conversation" starters:

"Somewhere, far off, a strange animal growled, startling him out of his daydreaming."

"He watched her move in front of him, her ass naturally swaying from side to side, even as she trudged up the steep trail."

"They were startled by the sudden appearance of another couple on the trail."

"The alpine lake spread out before them, inviting and sparkling as the sun began its slow descent behind the mountains."

"She looked at him with hunger in her eyes."

I LOVE YOU, DON'T TOUCH ME

Perhaps scouting out locations and muffling your moans aren't really the problems afoot amongst the flora and fauna. Maybe the issue is your lack of libido? Are you absolutely sick of him? Will he not leave you alone? Doesn't he know how you hate it when he's touchy-feely when you are all sweaty and gross?

Well, never fear. You can absolutely have some quiet time even if there are no doors to close or another room to go in. In fact, you're entitled to it. Keep these excuses handy when you are tempted to smack him over the head with the camp-stove skillet.

I'm feeling very spiritual. I need to meditate . . . over there.

I'm out of breath and can't really breathe with your tongue in my mouth right now.

I'm beat. I think I'm coming down with something, if my tingling lip is any indication.

I don't feel quite right. While it was delicious, I think your campfire con queso did a number on me.

I need to listen for wild animals. There are rumors that a cougar ate an eleven-year-old last month.

Shh, you'll scare the birds away. I've been waiting to see a
yellow-breasted sapsucker all day.

Can you keep watch? It'll be just like that Civil War camp
reenactment you participated in last month. I even brought
along hardtack!

How about I go forage for berries? I think they'd go well with
the dark chocolate I brought, which I know is your favorite.

I need to be alone right now to take in the beauty of our
surroundings.

Of course, you can resort to less-verbal methods when playing "Keep
Away." Nothing is less sexy than diarrhea.

- Rash
- Cold sore
- Excessive sweating
- Gas, and lots of it
- Halitosis
- Body odor
- Vomiting
- Fall asleep
- Snoring

Q&A, BABY

Okay, you're not sick of each other. In fact, you'd like to get even
closer. This is a perfect time, away from the maddening crowds and
the pressures of the day, to take your relationship to the next level,
or at least become more intimate. And I'm not talking about keeping
watch while the other relieves him- or herself.

Once you've got the camp set up, dinner and cleanup out of the
way, take time to focus on each other. Use the fact that you are out

of your normal setting and life to ask new questions and learn new things about each other.

Use your surroundings to inspire your line of questioning:

- 🍪 What's your favorite tree?
- 🍪 Describe your perfect day outdoors.
- 🍪 Have you ever been caught with your pants down? Would you like to be?
- 🍪 If you could wish upon a star, what would you wish for (besides more wishes)?
- 🍪 Were you ever dragged on camping trips as a kid?
- 🍪 Did you go to sleepaway camp? If so, tell me about it. Was it just like *Little Darlings*?
- 🍪 What do you consider "roughing it"?
- 🍪 What luxury item can you not live without?
- 🍪 What rustic item or activity do you secretly love?

Outdoor Aphrodisiacs

Oysters aren't the only things that will get your motor running. Here are a few other foods and beverages for your portable pantry that are thought to rev the engine. (Powdered rhinoceros horn has long been thought to be a crazy aphrodisiac but aside from the obvious drawbacks, it just doesn't really go that well with trail mix.) Caution: Don't eat these all at once. Your head (or something else) might explode.

✧ Almond	✧ Fig	✧ Pine nuts
✧ Avocado	✧ Ginger	✧ Pineapple
✧ Berries	✧ Honey	✧ Vanilla
✧ Chocolate	✧ Mustard	✧ Wine
✧ Carrot		

DIRTY TALK

Since you're dirty anyway, why not get really filthy in the forest? Dirty talk might not come easily to you, so start slow. You don't have to start in the dungeon with whips, chains, and leather corsets. Even dipping your toe into the dirty talk waters is going to be a refreshing and unexpected treat. And remember that you have a receptive (and captive) audience who's going to like anything you do.

So once you get warmed up and loosen your tongue, describe what you're doing in real time. Tell him how much you like stroking his arm or licking his chest. Ask him if he likes it. Ask him if he wants you to keep doing what you're doing.

Now take it a step further. Describe what you *want* to do to him. Again, ask him if he'd like it or like for you to do it. If you get a yes (and, um, you will), proceed to carry out your plan of attack.

Tell him how turned on you are. Tell him how attracted you are to him. Tell him how much you like looking at his body, both in and out of cargo shorts.

Now mix things up and tell him what you'd like him to do to you. If you're up for it, command him to please you. Give him specific direction. Be bossy. Don't worry if it feels weird at first. I guarantee you that you'll get used to it and, in fact, find that it comes naturally and feels pretty darn good.

Finally, use your surroundings. Rather than fantasize about being at a fancy costume ball or getting a happy ending on the massage table, talk about being lost in the woods with only each other for warmth. Or maybe you are in the surf making love, stopping only when the waiter wades up to you with a bucket of ice-cold beers. Or maybe you are forging through the jungle to discover a lost civilization. Whatever the case, use your backcountry locale to fuel your fantasies. You (and he) will be oh-so-glad you did.

Say My Name, Say My Name

What's your Grizzly Adams name? It's easy. Just pair your favorite trail snacklet with a wild animal.

trail snack + wild animal = your mountain moniker

For instance, would you be cherry cougar or chocolate warthog or Gatorade gopher? The possibilities are endless and let's face it, delicious.

Chapter 7

LET'S GET PHYSICAL

etties know how to get sweaty on a treadmill or even between the sheets. However, campin' cardio is a whole new ballgame. Actually, it's not a ballgame. There are no manicured fields or dugouts or men in snug white pants.

But I digress.

Working up a sweat in the wild can be one of nature's great gifts. The air smells a lot better than the dirty-sock aroma of your gym. The uneven ground or sand can work your glutes better than any Stairmaster. And as for the men, have you SEEN the hunky stubbly men in hiking boots and Columbia sportswear who are opting for a mountain bike or hike over a short walk to the couch (although that has its place, too)? *Seriously*.

Before you attempt to scale a mountain or even meander along a dirt trail with a slight grade (incline), you need to prep your body. And I'm not talking about a sugar scrub and cute cargo shorts. I'm talking about stretching and strength training, as distasteful as that sounds. I've barely gotten up a trail and rested on the shore of a crystalline alpine lake only to suck it on the way down because my joints were so stiff and sore. I had to sort of bounce from one straight leg to the other because my knees wouldn't bend. Don't let this happen to you! Pack some ibuprofen and, for your own sake, stretch, stretch like a cat. Not only is it embarrassing to be stuck, unable to power out of the wilderness under your own steam, but it's not exactly wise. If there's a storm brewing or darkness is approaching or you hear something rustling in the bushes, it behooves you to be able to hoof it out of there on your own.

Back to better Betty thoughts. Feel free to daydream about asking that lean rock climber at your local REI store to be your personal trainer. But in addition to some hands-on lunging, you also need to address some other, more necessary issues. Like, for instance, survival.

SURVIVAL TIPS

There's more to backcountry adventures than toting a backpack of snacks and hitting the trail in your cute rugged gear. In fact, if you take some precautions, you will be able to jauntily trek into the woods with the knowledge that you are being safe and responsible.

When heading into the wilderness, the first thing you should do is sign in at the trailhead. There is often a box, sheet, or bulletin board for you to do so. Carry a pen and paper (and even a push pin) in your glove compartment so you can write and post a short note, detailing your location, the number of your camping party, the time and date you set out, and when you expect to return. When you do return to the trailhead, be sure to remove the note if it's still there.

Clue someone in about your itinerary and be as detailed in your plans and location as possible. If anything should go wrong, specific directions and time frames will be helpful in securing assistance.

We've discussed protecting your food and locking down your waste by tying it up in a bear bag. It's not just environmentally sound, but it can save you from a mauling, not by Grizzly Adams, but by a grizzly bear. Put it up and away from your campsite.

STEP UP TO THE HIKE

Naturally, you're eager to get your show on the road, or hike on the trail. But take time to stretch properly. No matter how short the hike or level the trail, you will be challenged by the uneven terrain, switchbacks, and steep grades in both directions. Walking up an incline can be hard on a sidewalk in a hilly city so think about trekking on shifting sand, through heavily forested areas with thick roots snaking across the trail, or across deep snowdrifts. These may be extreme cases, but even with well-maintained trails that are easy to traverse, you will still want your muscles and joints warmed up and raring to go.

Before you even start, prevent blisters as best you can. The best way to do this is to wear properly fitting hiking boots—break them in before you go—and two layers of socks. To prevent chafing and wick away foot moisture and odor, slip on a thin sock liner and add a thick hiking sock on over that.

Reach for the Sky

When you are trekking uphill, you will be working your muscles. On the way down, your joints take a beating. Take care of both. Stretch thoroughly before you start your hike and if you have rested significantly before starting the decline, stretch again to loosen up muscles and tendons. Take ibuprofen as a preventative measure to alleviate joint pain and swelling. When it's safe to do so, walk with your hands above your head to avoid "sausage fingers" (when bodily fluids travel to the extremities).

Here is a good general warm-up routine for the wild. Work from the top down. Stand with your legs slightly apart and arms at your sides. With all of the following warm-ups, do them slowly and repeat six to ten times. Roll your head in gentle clockwise circles several times and then switch directions.

Now roll your shoulders up and back several times and then reverse directions. Raise your arms out at your sides to shoulder height and do arm circles in both directions. Isolate your torso and move that in gentle circles. Now work those hips like the rent is due! Don't forget your ankles; spend a good amount of time circling them both clockwise and counterclockwise.

It's important to spend some time warming up your gams. Put your hands at your sides and with a straight back, slowly squat to a sitting position while bringing your arms straight out in front of you to shoulder height. Slowly straighten your legs, feeling the burn in your quads and hamstrings. Repeat up to ten times. Do not rush. These are most effective when done slowly and with deliberation.

Now for another gym favorite: the lunge. With your hands on your hips, legs straight and slightly apart, take a big step forward with your right foot and slowly bend your right knee, taking care to keep your back straight and keeping your knee behind your toes. Sink into the stretch, keeping the back left foot stationary but bending the left leg as well. Now straighten your legs, bringing the right foot back to its original position. Now do the same lunge but with the left foot. Continue lunging with alternate legs for ten reps.

I know—this blows, right? Well, too bad. You'll pat yourself on the back later for being so limber and pliable. Here's a stretch that feels fantastic on your calves: Facing a car or tree, place your palms against it, keeping your back and arms straight, legs shoulder width apart. Lean against the car or tree and bend your right leg. Straighten and stretch the left leg behind you, with the toes of your foot on the ground and pressing your heel toward the ground until you feel the stretch. Bring the left foot back to its original position and switch legs, alternating and repeating ten times.

Now stretch your shin. Put the toes of one foot against a tire, wall, or thick tree, keeping the heel on the ground. The other foot should be flat on the ground and bearing the bulk of your weight. Keeping your back straight, lean your body into the stretch toward the tire/wall/tree to loosen up the front of your calf. When done, repeat with the other shin.

Do you have any particular problem areas? If so, research a few exercises beforehand so you make sure to warm up and stretch those areas thoroughly. If you have a tight IT band, for instance, there are a couple of great exercises that will stretch your hips and the sides of your thighs. Get stitches in your side? Spend more time stretching your torso. Reach your arms over your head and then, bending at the waist first to one side and then the other, stretch your sides and arms as far as possible.

PREP SCHOOL

While it's important to start your wilderness grooming well ahead of your trip, there are a few other things you may want to consider as well before leaving civilization behind.

Be honest with yourself. If you haven't seen the inside of a gym since Britney Spears was considered a normal Southern girl, don't agree on a vigorous three-day excursion into the heart of darkness. You'll slow the Iron Johns down and could perhaps feel chagrined at your limitations.

Research where you're going. Don't just leave the navigation and mapping to your partner. At least ask him to show you the planned route and learn how to use a compass. And once you can determine east from west, make sure you actually pack a compass. And please, check the weather forecast before you head out. Know when the sun rises and more importantly, when it sets. You don't want to be caught away from your camp or your car as it's getting dark and cold. You want to be snuggled in your tent with your boy as it's getting dark and cold.

Team up for your wilderness excursion with at least one other person, preferably two. If someone bites it on the trail and twists her ankle, a pal can stay with her while the other seeks a hunky hiker to assist.

TRACKING YOUR POSITION

Before you head into the outdoors, you should know where you're going, even after you go off the grid. That means knowing how to read a topographic map and compass.

First of all, it's essential to know that the magnetic north on a compass is different from true north on a map. The difference is called *declination*. Some compasses take this into account and correct for it, which is a good thing since you have to figure this out when tracking your position.

To locate your position in the wilderness, spot a landmark and find it on your map. Aim your compass arrow at the landmark, turning the dial so that the north on the dial lines up with the needle pointing to magnetic north on your compass.

Read the bearing at the arrow. Add or subtract the degrees of declination—don't worry, this isn't rocket science. Your map should list the declination conversion. Follow directions on your compass for conversion. If you have a basic compass, manually adjust it: turn the dial clockwise the correct number of degrees for west declination, counterclockwise for east declination.

Place your compass over your map, align the compass with the landmark, and turn the compass so that the north on the dial matches the north on the map. Draw a line—your position is on this bearing.

Now repeat this process with a second landmark. Your position is at the point where the lines intersect. Cool, huh? Learn more at *www .learn-orienteering.org/old.*

You can also use nature to determine your position. In most parts of the Northern Hemisphere, moss grows on the north side of trees. And remember that the sun rises in the east and sets in the west. You just have to know what general direction you came from or want to go.

TIP: Carry a cell phone. It takes up space but it can serve as a homing device if you are lost in the wild. Although you might not be able to make a call, "pings" off of towers can assist in giving your location to searchers should you lose your way.

THE TRAIL MIX

There's more to hiking than just navigating the trail and breathing in the crisp air, although those are key components. There is quite a bit of trail etiquette to display to fellow hikers and to your environment. I know, it sounds a bit out there, but while you are outward bound, you need to be as courteous as if you were a houseguest at Windsor Castle. The good news is that you don't have to curtsey or write a thank-you note.

Don't wander off the trails. Aside from minimizing your impact on the environment (this is the one time you don't want to make a dramatic entrance), staying on the trail will reduce the chances of getting lost or hurt. If you or your campanions have a pooch you want to bring along, check local regulations. Dogs are illegal in many state and all national parks. Check one of the many excellent websites that detail national, state, and beach regulations regarding dogs. If you do bring your dog, keep him on a leash during your entire adventure so that he doesn't disturb other hikers, wildlife, or the foliage. Take into consideration the terrain, which can hurt a dog's paw pads if you take a long hike and he isn't used to it.

Observe signs and trail markers. They are there for a reason.

And when you are ready to take a break—perhaps at a glorious scenic overlook or on a large rock next to an aqua-colored lake—step away from the trail or the most desirable viewing area. While it's a lovely idea to enjoy lunch next to a waterfall, don't hog the space and prevent others from enjoying the view or snapping photos. While the cascading water does frame you nicely, make other hikers work to take your photo. Don't give it away for free!

While on the subject of trail hogging, keep your group small. If you've got a large party of backpackers, split into groups of four or fewer while day hiking. Hike single file and keep a good distance between you and the peeps in front of and behind you. Ask your guy to lead the way; your view will be spectacular, and I'm not talking about the surroundings.

As a Betty, you're already nice so it shouldn't be too hard to be courteous in the wilderness. But when you are hot, sweaty, and bushed, you may not be so delightful when a burly hiker happens across your path. No matter your mood, yield to others on the trail, particularly those climbing uphill (they have the right-of-way). If you suspect you'll get surly or you just want to be alone with your campanions, schedule your hike or trip during less-popular times of the year or day.

And when you are tempted to sound your barbaric yawp, keep it to yourself. You could disturb the reverie of other hikers and alert wildlife to your presence. Again, this is not the time to be making a dramatic entrance, especially if there are bears, cougars, or other critters with sharp teeth lurking about.

Whenever possible, travel on established trails and durable surfaces. While there may not be concrete sidewalks, you can choose to walk on rock, gravel, or packed dirt and forego trampling over wildflowers and the like. And if you come across something interesting, such as old railroad ties or an indigenous people's abode, take the same approach as you do when checking out your friend's tasty new boyfriend: look but don't touch. And never pick flowers or collect rocks or shells, no matter how lovely they are. Take a picture instead; it may not last longer but it can be a lovely souvenir of your trip.

FIRST AID

No one anticipates cutting, burning, spraining, or otherwise injuring themselves, but it's been known to happen to the graceful and clumsy alike. So don't think you're above the fray and leave your first-aid kit in your medicine cabinet. Here's the absolute minimum you should bring with you into the backcountry for short hikes.

- Antiseptic wipes and ointment
- Bandages
- First-aid tape
- Gauze (to tape a sprain, apply compression)
- Bio-occlusive dressing, such as Tegaderm (a thin, clear dressing that allows a wound to breathe while protecting it)
- Ibuprofen (general pain reliever and good for joint aches)
- Anti-itching lotion
- Moleskin (great for blisters)
- Small pair of scissors or multipurpose pocketknife
- Tweezers

NOTE: A lot of mishaps can befall you in the backcountry, so it's a good idea to read up on first aid and bring along a guidebook. We cover only the Betty basics here. And if you are camping for more than a day or two, bring a more extensive first-aid kit. Many outdoor shops sell good portable kits.

A Blister in the Sun

Blisters are the bane of a hiker's existence and the best way to deal with them is to go on the offensive. To prevent them, wear serious hiking socks, preferably with a thin, moisture-wicking liner, and make sure your hiking boots fit properly and are broken in.

If you do sense any chafing, run the risk of looking like a wuss and take a break to check it out. If there is reddened skin, cover the area with a generous piece of adhesive.

If you get an honest-to-goodness blister, don't pop it. Leave it be. If it breaks, trim off the excess skin, irrigate and clean the area, and apply moleskin or a thick bandage over the blister. Think of your blister as a badge of honor rather than a total drag on the ticket.

Bite Me

Love bites are one thing, nasty insect or critter bites are another thing altogether. They blemish the skin, sure, but they can also be uncomfortable or dangerous. Steer clear of all wildlife and tie up your food properly.

No matter what kind of critter lights into you, it's important to clean the area using basic wound care.

- Purify water
- Wash your hands
- Irrigate the wound thoroughly with the purified water
- Clean with an antibacterial cleanser and follow with an antibacterial ointment or cream
- Bandage the wound
- Check for infection
- Change the dressing as needed

IF IT'S A BUG BITE

Clean the area, apply a cold compress to reduce swelling, take ibuprofen, apply an antibacterial cream or anti-itching lotion such as calamine. Refrain from scratching, but you already know that.

IF IT'S A TICK

Check your skin regularly since ticks take their time when burrowing into your sweet Betty skin. To remove a tick, grasp it as close to your skin as possible with tweezers, and pull slowly and steadily. If you do this too fast or jerkily, you can cause the tick to salivate or regurgitate infected fluids. Not only does this sound gross, it's dangerous as well. It's important to make sure you remove the tick's head completely to avoid infection. Once removed, clean the area as you would any wound.

IF YOU ARE BITTEN BY A SNAKE

You might have been envenomated (yeah, it doesn't sound good because it isn't good). Irrigate and clean the wound. You can try using a mechanical suction device (do not use your mouth, even if you remember Nancy Drew doing this successfully). Apply light compression with an elastic band, immobilize the limb to prevent the toxin from spreading, and make the bitten campanion rest. Seek help immediately if the symptoms seem major. If the symptoms are minor or nonexistent after 30 to 60 minutes, you should still evacuate with the injured person to get the bite checked.

IF A MAMMAL TAKES A BITE OUT OF YOU

Many animals have a load of bacteria lurking in their mouths, so it's paramount to irrigate and clean the wound with purified water. Apply pressure to stop any bleeding, dress the wound, elevate the injured area above heart level, and seek medical help immediately. The injured person should receive a rabies shot (or shots) upon returning to civilization.

Basic Training

If someone in your party is injured, take a nod from airline safety. Assist yourself first before helping others. Make sure that you can get to your campanions safely; you can't help them if you are mired in quicksand, twist your own ankle, or fall off a cliff. Take a deep breath and a moment to collect your thoughts before rushing to someone's side. Stay cool even if it's hot outside. If it's you who is injured, bummer. Follow the same logic. Stay still and take a moment to assess what hurts and how badly before attempting to move. When you do go into action, move slowly and deliberately.

Now, you probably were looking for a reason to feel up your campanion. If he is injured, now's your chance. Check for cuts, abrasions, lumps, tenderness, swelling, numbness, odd coloring, basically anything that feels wrong. Perform a ten-point check on the body in this order:

- Scalp
- Face and eyes
- Ears and nose
- Neck
- Chest and sides
- Abdomen
- Pelvis
- Arms and legs
- Back
- Buttocks

If you discover a cut or open wound, apply pressure (with a clean cloth) until the bleeding stops, irrigate and clean the wound (using purified water), and then dress it with a gauze or bandage.

Look for signs of shock. The injured person may feel weak; have a weak, rapid pulse; and clammy, pale skin. Place the victim on his or her back, put a pillow or padding under the head, and keep your campanion as warm and dry as possible. Hydrate and offer a pain reliever.

If you fear a serious injury, do not attempt to move the person but seek help immediately. Ideally, there are at least three in your group, so there is a campanion to stay with the patient and another to hightail it back to civilization for assistance. Even though you may be distracted, take care to note the injured party's position so you can return quickly to the site.

Mountain High

The air is thin at 10,000 feet. If you are hiking in the mountains, be aware that you might become light-headed and short of breath in a way that your trainer back at sea level could never make you.

Acclimatize, which is a fancy pants word for getting used to higher altitudes gradually. Start your adventure and spend your first night below 10,000 feet. Climb no higher than 1,000 feet per day, taking a day to rest every 3,000 feet. If you do find yourself getting wifty, rest, hydrate, and eat something. It's common sense, right? And if the symptoms lurk about, just return to a lower elevation.

If you do return to a lower elevation and symptoms still persist (loss of appetite, weakness, fatigue, apathy, dizziness, swollen face, headache, nausea, shortness of breath), assess the affected person's ability to hike down unassisted. Whether you help her down or she takes her time hiking down on her own, she should get back to a reasonable elevation and seek medical help. If there are more than two of you, one should go for help and the other should stay with the affected person.

That's Cold

Don't think that you only need to worry about cold temperatures in the winter. If you are in the mountains, the temperatures can dip quite low at night and even during daylight hours at the height of summer.

Make sure you bring along a lot of layers of clothing and outerwear. And put them on before you get cold or wet. It's much harder to warm up or dry off once you're chilled. Seek shelter, keep your body moving, drink fluids, and eat carbs to stave off hypothermia and frostbite. Build a fire if you are in serious trouble (see page 82 for information on how to do this safely).

Some signs of mild hypothermia include:

- Shivering
- Cool, pale skin (think vampire)
- Weariness and a lethargic pace
- Lack of coordination
- Jerky movements
- Poor judgment (hooking up with a gamey mountain man doesn't count)
- Confusion
- Nausea

If the person is unable to walk, cannot talk, stops shivering and develops rigidity of muscles, and perhaps loses consciousness, they are moving from mild to moderate hypothermia and you should seek immediate medical help. If he does go into shock and becomes unconscious, he could have severe hypothermia and die. Skin will be blue and cold, and he could go into cardiopulmonary arrest. Scary, right? Pack the appropriate gear, check the weather report, and make sure this doesn't happen.

Then there's frostbite. This nasty condition freezes your tissues—fingers, toes, nose, and anything that protrudes from your body are particularly vulnerable. Frostbite starts out by rendering your bits and pieces red, numb, painful, and swollen before turning white and grayish and then cold, hard, insensitive, and blistered. It basically kills tissue, and you run the risk of losing frostbitten areas. Treat frostbitten areas as soon as possible by immersing in hot water (104 degrees F). Do not rub the affected area or put the person near a fire. After rewarming the area, pad, immobilize, and elevate it. If you have anti-inflammatory medication, now's the time to use it. If it's the feet that are frozen and you still are deep in the backcountry, leave them be. Seriously. It's possible to walk on frostbitten feet, but it would be hella painful to walk on thawed tootsies, and more damage can be done if there is a danger of refreezing.

The Heat Is On

Nasty sunburns are not the only thing you need to worry about on hot, sunny days. While the weather may seem perfect, it can lead to heat exhaustion, heat stroke, and dehydration.

Drink plenty of water (or sport drink or oral rehydration solution), wear light-colored clothing, avoid hiking during the hottest times of day, chill out in the shade.

Watch for signs of nausea, vomiting, faintness, thirst, disorientation, dizziness, and a rapid pulse. While a challenging hike could produce many of these symptoms in an out-of-shape Betty, all of them together on a steaming hot day could be signs of something more serious. Seek shade, drink fluids (if you can, sport drinks that contain electrolytes), and do whatever you can to bring down the body temperature.

Poison Oak, Ivy, and Sumac

While some three-leaf plants soothe the soul, steer clear of them in the wilderness. Poison oak, ivy, and sumac are laced with poisonous sap, known as urushiol, in the leaves, stems, and roots. If you become contaminated and know it, wash your skin thoroughly and immediately. If you don't notice, your skin will start itching, and

badly. It will become inflamed and possibly blister. Once you are infected, the only way to treat it is to use calamine lotion on the affected area or soak in Epsom salts and wait it out. But it's not contagious so don't fear treating your campanion's nasty outbreak. Just play Nurse Betty.

THE WILD WORKOUT

Below are a few considerations for popular outdoor activities. By no means is this the be-all-and-end-all guide for specific outdoor activities (what I could say about spelunking could fill its own Betty book!). I just want to offer a few tips to think about before you leave the REI store.

Swimming

No matter how cool and inviting a body of water looks after a hellacious hike, don't jump in feet first. Check out how deep the water is. If it's a river or body of fast-moving water, check the current and don't stray too far from the riverbank or shore. You could get caught in the current, riptide, or hydraulic. And who knows if that current is going to carry you to a waterfall or rocky area. Speaking of rocky, don't walk into the middle of a river, even if it only comes up to your knees. Your feet could get caught or lodged in the uneven rocky riverbed.

The water could also be polluted if it has a river or stream feeding into it from a far-off civilized, eco-hating land. The more likely scenario in the backcountry is that your cool drink of water is home to a variety of fish and water-loving creatures. Refrain from bathing with soap and shampoo in fresh or saltwater and don't whoop it up with your friends. You might scare off the fish, which you might appreciate in the short-term, since nothing strange will brush up against you in the water. But in the long-term, you could upset the ecosystem and do you really want that on your conscience?

Confine your water play to short periods of time. You don't want to spook wildlife that may depend on it for food or water.

Water Sports

While on the subject of all things wet, if you are kayaking or rafting in the backcountry, get yourself a river guide if you aren't experienced. Before strapping on a personal floatation device (PFD), stretch and warm up your body. Your upper body (arms and shoulders) will certainly be working hard as you paddle or row, but don't ignore your abs and legs. Rowing and paddling take a toll on your abdominals, and rafting requires you to use your leg muscles to hold you securely in the inflatable.

Pick the right raft or kayak for your outing. Two-person kayaks are great as they allow you to be social and double up on the manpower. Inflatable, self-bailing rafts are ideal for groups of four or more. Inner tubes are best for floating lazily down a slow-moving river with no rocks and lots of beer.

Study the route you plan to take. Most navigable rivers have maps you can review to determine the best course. It's also a good idea to pull your raft up on a riverbank and scout out nasty white water on foot before taking the plunge. You've seen *The River Wild*, haven't you? Meryl Streep is one bad Betty, but even she knew to plan out her trip before entering the Gauntlet.

Mountain Biking

Pack water bottle, air pump, repair kit, snacks, and basic first aid. Check your bike and your gear thoroughly. Before you do this, however, check that bikes are allowed on your selected trail. Look online at the many mountain biking sites or at the relevant local, state, or national park website. Make sure your tire pressure and seat position and height are correct for mountain terrains. Wear elbow and knee pads, gloves, a well-padded pair of shorts, and don't forget your helmet, no matter how distasteful the idea of hat head is.

Stretch your legs and arms before climbing on your bike. Ride on open trails, control your bike (that is, refrain from careening willy-nilly down a path), and respect the Leave No Trace ethic. Alert other hikers, bikers, and horseback riders on the trail to your presence. Slow down when others are near, as well as when you are approaching turns or blind spots. Refrain from biking on wet trails; you can damage your bike, the trail, and yourself, as the conditions are more treacherous. Yield to others on the trail and if you are biking downhill, get off your bike and pull over if you meet others riding or even hiking uphill.

Rock Climbing

Climbing is terrific exercise and it can be an extremely social activity, filled with lots of hunky mountain men. It might be worth spending some time doing arm curls and lunges so you can join them on the rock. While it may seem at first blush that your arms will be doing all the work (after all, it's called climbing), you should let your legs do as much of the work as you can when rock climbing. You should be in good physical condition, with decent upper body strength.

When first learning rock climbing, take a lesson with an experienced climber and practice at an indoor climbing wall. More than most sports, rock climbing requires gear—ropes, helmet, carabiners, for starters—and requires that you thoroughly check your gear. Your life can depend on it.

Choose an approved climbing route that will not disturb birds and other wildlife. When first learning how to climb, look for short routes that allow you to rest on ledges between climbing areas.

Spelunking

Heading underground? Like rock climbing, make sure you are with an experienced guide and thoroughly check your gear. Study up or take a class if you can. Make sure your electric headlamp is in good working order and squirrel away two other light sources on your person, as well as batteries and spare parts. Outfit yourself with a helmet with chinstrap (I know, not cute, but we are talking about safety here), gloves, knee pads, bag for waste (again, not sexy but necessary), food, and water.

Layer your clothing, as it can be quite cold underground and you can even be susceptible to hypothermia. Head down below with a group of four to six, and as with any backcountry trip, let someone know of your whereabouts, and when you plan to leave and return.

And it may be obvious, but think about any fears you have of being in the dark, enclosed spaces, or underground. If you have a severe case of achluophobia (fear of the dark), for instance, you may want to wait at the mouth of the cave.

Winter in the Backcountry

Snowshoeing sounds like fun (even though you might look like you're wearing clown shoes). It can be . . . if you prepare. Before you head out, make sure there's enough snow to warrant your outing. Check the weather report, as well as the time of sunset. Study the trail you plan to take, as it's easy to get confused when the terrain is covered by snow. Stretch out your legs. Look for packed, flat trails when starting out to get the blood flowing and the hang of it. Dress in several light layers that you can peel off and put on as you heat up or cool off.

For snowshoeing, take small, natural steps. Don't look down and do your best not to step on the tails of your snowshoes while walking. Hiking poles work great in tandem with snowshoes.

When it comes to cross-country skiing, try to keep your body loose and gliding, and match your body's movement to your breathwork. If you have ever exercised on a cross-country ski machine at the gym, you get the idea. You are aiming for a diagonal stride, where your arms and legs are moving in a scissor-like coordination.

Take turns breaking the trail. The lead person has the hardest job, so periodically switch the single-file order of campanions to share the load. And with any activity, plan a time to stop or return to camp so you have tasty vittles to look forward to and dream about while you are puffing away and working up a sweat.

Avalanche Tips

Avalanches are a real and present danger in wintry backcountry. Here are just a few tips to keep you safe, but if you are planning on traveling into snowy mountain areas, familiarize yourself thoroughly with avalanche risks and self-rescue techniques.

- ✦ Plan your route and check the weather report in advance
- ✦ Avoid mountainous areas after heavy snowfall or prolonged periods of high wind
- ✦ Check out the terrain: steep slopes, smooth open slopes, and leeward slopes can all be dangerous and contain unstable slabs of snow
- ✦ Travel on ridge tops and the windward side of a mountain
- ✦ Don't hike below steep open slopes, especially during warming periods or when it's raining or snowing heavily
- ✦ If there is any doubt as to the weather and terrain, cancel the trip or plan a different route
- ✦ Do not travel alone
- ✦ You and your campanions should spread out when hiking through avalanche backcountry

Chapter 8

......

THE WILD LIFE

s if dealing with dirt and trees and plants and pollen weren't enough, communing with nature also means coexisting outdoors with wild animals, and I'm not talking about your campanion who likes to drink a bit too much Jagermeister for her (and your) own good. The forest, jungle, even desert are brimming with wildlife. Birds and bats and bears, oh my, call the great outdoors home. You are an uninvited house guest, and you should take care not to piss off or disturb your hosts. Most animals, if you are respectful, will not mind the intrusion. In fact, you probably won't even see them, as they are shy when it comes to bipedal Betties.

But these days, civilization has encroached on wildlife, and some critters have become more aggressive, especially when there's food around. Why work to find dinner when there's a cooler chock-full of tasty vittles? Just like the signs at the zoo, do not feed the animals (even birds)—you can disrupt the ecosystem and leave wildlife wanting more from the next group of unsuspecting campers. In fact, you should pretty much steer clear of animals altogether. Don't try to attract that adorable bunny or call out a mating cry to a yellow-bellied sapsucker. Admire them quietly as you move on. It's far too easy to step smack-dab into a nest or den, confuse a baby, or rile up a protective mama. Even if the animal is a docile herbivore like Bambi, it's always best to leave it be. Skirt water sources where wildlife might drink or seek out food; don't make them skittish to take a drink. They are probably already edgy about the other critters in the woods, so don't add to their stress.

I don't mean to scare you. Going into the backcountry should be an adventure, not a scary, cautionary tale. However, a little planning and care go a long way toward making sure you (and your food) are safe and the indigenous fauna are fat and happy.

As with plants, it's helpful to know what animals you should give a wide berth and those you should just ignore. This chapter will introduce you to a host of wild beasts (but not wildebeests) and give you a few suggestions for how to deal with them should you encounter them on the trail.

THE ANIMAL KINGDOM

In thinking about wildlife, I'm reminded of my favorite bumper sticker: "If God didn't want us to eat animals, why'd he make them out of meat?" I think some carnivorous critters would ask the same question.

Let's break backcountry animals into two categories: the carnivores and the herbivores. Like carne asada, carnivores are all about meat. And carnivore moms are all about their kids. Stay away from nests and dens, no matter how cute and cuddly a creature may be.

Omnivores aren't picky. They'll eat whatever they can get their hands or paws on (that is, they eat both flora and fauna). But while they don't sound as ominous as carnivores, they can be just as dangerous.

Herbivores focus their feeding on plant life and vegetation. You don't have to worry about these animals preying on you for your tasty body, but you should still give them a wide berth. Any animal will attack if it feels cornered or threatened.

Before we get to know a bit about individual creatures great and small, there are a few general rules to dealing safely with wild animals.

Observe wildlife from a distance. Do not follow or approach an animal, no matter how cute or benign it may seem. Yes, that includes Bambi and Thumper.

Steer clear of wildlife during sensitive times, such as mating season, nesting season, when they are raising young, or during winter.

Vore-acious: An Incomplete List

Carnivores	Herbivore	Omnivore
Mountain lion	Deer	Bear
Bobcat	Moose	Pig
Coyote	Cow	Raccoon
Wolf	Sheep	Opossum
Eagles and falcons	Rabbit	Fox
Hyena	Antelope	Chicken
Sea lion	Squirrel	
Seal	Mouse	
Crocodile		

Avoid wildlife during *your* sensitive time. If you can schedule your trip around your period, do it. Some women have even suppressed their periods by starting a new pack of birth control pills and skipping the pills that they take during their period week.

Never, ever feed the animals.

So let's check out a few of the furry fellas (aside from your own bearded boy who likes bear hugs) you might find in the forest and how to deal effectively and safely with them.

Bears

Even if you've never seen one in real life, you should know a bear when you see one. Big, check. Furry, check. Huge paws, check. Sharp teeth, uh, crap, check. I hope you don't run into one, figuratively and definitely literally, but if you do, do not run. As fleet of foot as you may be, a bear is faster. No matter its size, a bear can *move*.

So if you are in bear country, tear your eyes away from your guy's backside and keep an eye out for signs of bear activity (tracks or scat). If you see paw prints, note that grizzly claws extend farther away from the pads than black bears.' Scat (feces) will be greater than 2 inches in diameter.

Bears will usually hightail it out of the area if they sense your presence. If the wind is at your back, they might pick up your scent. If the wind is hitting you in the face, your chances of an encounter increase.

It's an excellent idea to carry a bear deterrent spray when in bear country. But don't tuck it into your pack; keep it close at hand. When a bear starts moving toward you, you'll panic and you won't have time to fish out the spray.

Steer clear of any sort of animal carcass; a bear can feast on that for days. Confine your hiking to daylight hours; grizzlies are most active at dawn, dusk, and nighttime.

• • • • • • • • • • • • • Bear Body Language • • • • • • • • • • • • • •

Stands on its hind feet:	trying to get a good look and smell, as he may be unsure of what's in front of him (you *are* pretty unique)
Swings its head or turns sideways from you:	trying to find a way out of the situation (much like you on your last date); he doesn't want to charge
Looks you in the eyes with ears cocked back:	you are too close and he does not like it (he could also bark, woof, or moan to drive home the point; in this case, moaning is not a good thing)
Pops its jaws:	no, he doesn't have a bad case of TMJ; he's agitated and ready to charge (maybe a bluff charge)
Charges and knocks you down:	wants to remove a perceived threat (he wants to be the most fabulous creature in the backcountry)

Take preventative measures: cook well away from your tent and water sources (200 feet for the latter) and securely tie up your food (see page 75). Speaking of being tied up, keep your pooch on a leash and children close by.

If you do encounter a bear, stand your ground and do not make eye contact. If you are a good distance away, talk normally and wave your arms so it can recognize you as human, not dinner. If it doesn't make a move, bow your head or do whatever you can do to assume a submissive position. Back away slowly.

If the bear charges, reach for your deterrent spray and aim for its eyes (try to spray with the wind, not into it, to avoid being blinded by the spray). Once you've hit your mark, don't push your luck. Get the heck out of there.

If your luck has run out and the bear makes contact, lie face down, legs spread apart, and protect your neck and face. Keep your pack on. Do your best not to move or make a sound. The bear may lose interest in you if you play opossum (just like when you are trying to deter an overzealous date). If the bear continues to maul you, fight back and go for the head and eyes.

Mountain Lions

The largest cats in North America, mountain lions (also cougars, panthers, pumas) are pretty sly. They often live and lurk in areas with a lot of unsuspecting prey and places to hide. But when it comes to humans, they will try to avoid a confrontation and will look for escape routes. Let them!

It may seem obvious but do not approach a mountain lion. Don't run pell-mell in the opposite direction either. They are predators and running may fuel the desire to chase. And I don't care if you have a gold medal in sprinting, a mountain lion is going to catch you. So, take a deep breath, stand tall, face the beast, and look it in the eye. Do everything you can to be tall and big. While you may have picked your clothing to appear slim despite your many layers, now is not the time to channel Nicole Richie. Puff yourself up, raise up your arms, wave them, speak in a loud, firm voice. Throw stones and branches if you can do so without bending over or crouching, which will make you look like four-legged prey.

A mountain lion isn't used to your size and shape, and if you display large and loud behavior, it might feel that you are a threat to it. If it does attack, remain standing, protect your head and neck, and fight back with whatever you can, aiming for its eyes and throat.

While they don't relish chomping on you, pets are another story and a good reason to keep your pup on a leash. Your cocker spaniel is easy pickins for a mountain lion, especially if she's bounding through the backcountry, barking and exploring. She may whine if you keep her leashed, but at least she won't be dinner. Similarly, keep small children close to you at all times.

Mountain lions are large, muscular cats and can weigh up to 200 pounds. They live in the wild in the Western and Southwestern United States but have a widespread distribution in the Western Hemisphere. So you could pretty much run into them anywhere in the backcountry. They are more active at dawn and dusk, so confining your activities to daylight hours is a wise idea.

Cougars kill by stalking their prey about 30 feet away and then pouncing from a hiding place, going for the neck. As if they aren't fearsome enough, cougars do not roar like you'd think. Rather, they make bird-like chirping sounds and a whistling sound. I saw *Jurassic Park* and this kind of noise reminds me of raptors, nasty pieces of work. Before you leave on your backcountry trek, check with local authorities to see if mountain lions frequent the area. Plan your activities accordingly and refrain from bending over.

Coyotes

Like other predators (and let's face it, party Betties), coyotes are most active during early morning, late evening, and nighttime. If they are in really remote areas or in cool climates, they might be seen throughout the day.

Don't feed coyotes (duh!), and make sure you tie up your food and trash securely.

Keep pets close at hand and on a leash. If you've got kids with you, keep them on a short leash as well.

Coyotes can adapt to a variety of terrains and climates and survive on whatever food they can scare up, which can include rabbits, mice, birds, young deer, and sheep. Much like that twerp assistant of yours, a coyote loses its fear of people quickly and can become bold and aggressive. If you do run into a cheeky coyote, use negative reinforcement to let it know that there's no room at the inn for the likes of it. Throw rocks, make loud noises, douse them with water, anything to let a coyote know it should be afraid, very afraid.

Bobcats

As magnetic and fascinating as you are, bobcats are just not that into you. Don't take it personally; they pretty much steer clear of all people. However, like mountain lions, if they feel cornered or threatened, they can become aggressive and dangerous. Cut a wide berth around them, give them avenues of escape, and like coyotes, offer negative reinforcement. Shine your flashlights, throw stones, make some noise, puff yourself up. Do whatever you can to run them off without running away yourself. Remember, predators may be stimulated by the sight of you hurriedly fleeing the scene.

Raccoons

Yes, they're adorable, but, like that guy you dated with the picture of his mom on his desktop, they can be bad news beneath their endearing exteriors. You can contract rabies or roundworms by contact with this little bandit. Don't feed a raccoon, and make sure you tie up your food and trash (sound familiar?). The same strategy goes for opossums and skunks. You certainly don't want your campsite to get skunked by a scared critter looking for a snack.

Rabbits and Deer

Like that fantastic-looking chocolate pagoda you ordered at the new fusion restaurant last week, some things *are* as sweet as they seem at first blush. Rabbits and deer look cute and they act cute. Don't be afraid. But don't treat them like a domesticated animal. Do not pat the bunny, do not approach Bambi, do not try to feed or water the walking plush toy. Admire it from a distance and allow it to hop along.

Wolves

Predators who run in packs, wolves are found in Alaska, Montana, Wyoming, and Idaho, as well as Great Lake states like Michigan, Minnesota, and Wisconsin. They can range in color from gray to black to all white. They are pretty adaptable, and live in a variety of environments—woods, tundra, desert, mountains—so you should be on guard in various backcountry situations. They snack on large hooved animals such as deer, moose, and elk, as well as smaller mammals such as beavers and rabbits. Resist the urge to save the cute animal, and leave natural selection to do its business.

Wolves communicate by howling, body and facial expressions, and scent markings. If you sense wolves in the area or encounter a wolf, follow the same advice as when dealing with mountain lions. Make yourself as big as possible, stand tall, make noise and throw objects to chase off the wolf. Do not run; rather, calmly back away maintaining eye contact all the while. In general, wolves fear people, so maintain a general attitude of strength (and keep your dog by your side on a leash, for goodness sake!).

Javelinas

Javelinas are sort of like prickly wild boars. They travel in groups of five to fifteen and have migrated from the jungles of South America to the arid Southwest United States. Like many animals, they prefer to root out their food in the early hours of the morning and the waning hours of the evening. They dig roots, nuts, fruit, that sort of thing, but can hold their own against smaller predators. They'll ignore you if you do the same, so don't be freaked out by their long tusks. Move along and let them have that wild blackberry bush.

Snakes

Like George Hamilton, snakes love hot, sunny weather. They will often sun themselves on empty trails or roads. The heat regulates their cold-blooded bodies. If you run into a snake coiled up or slithering on the trail, calmly back away. Stay on established trails; you have a better chance of scouting a snake ahead of you. Wear long pants and closed-toe shoes (you should be wearing hiking boots in the backcountry, anyway). If you are bitten by a venomous snake (which is rare and rarely fatal), seek medical attention immediately. Without going after it, try to identify the snake, so you can receive the correct antivenom.

Keep as still as possible (which is hard, considering you want to haul ass to the emergency room), and keep the bitten area just below your heart level. Remove any items that may restrict circulation to the bitten area. Watches and shoes may become problematic and uncomfortable as the area swells. Wrap a bandage (called a constriction band) a few inches above the bite, but keep it loose enough that blood can flow to the area. You should be able to fit a finger under the bandage. Do not eat or drink anything; do not take any pain medication.

If you have a snakebite kit handy, wash the bite and place the suction device over the affected area. Do not suck the poison out with your mouth!

Seals and Sea Lions

Sea lions and seals split their time between the ocean and the shore. If you spot one on the beach, do not touch or feed the animal. Don't try to return it to the water. It may be resting or feeling ill. The best thing to do is make a note of its location, as well as observe its overall condition (Is it thin? What's its size, length, color? Does the animal have any special markings or injuries?). Then report your findings to the authorities, so they can take the proper steps to ensure the best care for the animal. Remember, these are wild animals with teeth, so keep ample distance from the beached beast.

Moose, Elk, Reindeer, and Caribou

Members of the deer family, moose, elk, and caribou feed on grasses and woody plants and can live in a variety of habitats, including forests, meadows, deserts, and snow-covered mountains, although they tend to gravitate toward the colder mountain regions of North America and Europe. While large (moose can weigh up to 1600 pounds), they are not aggressive in general but can become dangerous if surprised or protecting their young. Regardless, leave them alone and admire them from a distance, as they can attract the attention of mountain lions, bears, wolves, and coyotes.

Jellyfish

If you are going to encounter the beach in the backcountry, you may also cross paths with jellyfish. They are jelly-like (though some look like egg yolks) and have almost invisible tentacles filled with stinging cells that erupt and release a toxin on contact. Similarly, Portuguese man-of-wars, are a group of organisms that share a gas-filled float. They too, have long tentacles filled with stinging cells.

During certain times of year, jellyfish and man-of-wars can be blown into the surf and onto the beach, making it easy for you to get stung. As soon as you are stung, use an anti-itch lotion and stay out of the surf. Move your blanket farther up the beach.

Stingrays

Stingrays (the animal, not the car) present another hazard of the splashing in the surf. Cool and aerodynamic with their flat wings, stingrays have been known to hang out in shallow waters, and a sting—which comes from a razor-sharp barb at the base of its tail—can be dangerous and even deadly. They release a toxic venom when they sting. You can get stung by stepping on a stingray so the best way to avoid an injury is to shuffle your feet in the surf, rather than taking normal steps. This will make it more likely that you bump into, rather than step on, the stingray. Wearing sneakers or footwear is also advisable. If you are stung, get out of the water and seek medical attention immediately.

Bats

No need to describe what a bat looks like; you've most likely seen at least one vampire movie. Mammals, they can carry rabies, and a bite or scratch may be so small that you don't detect it immediately. Most bats subsist on insects, a few go for fruit, and only three species (out of 1,100) fancy blood. They only come out in the dark so chances are slim that you'll encounter one up close. Don't try to prove that you're a big, brave Betty. Avoid bats and if one or several fly toward you, stay low and cover your head.

Bird-watching: A Primer

If you are interested in doing a bit of birding while you're exploring the backcountry, there are a few things to keep in mind:

- ✧ Pack portable binoculars, a small bird identification guide, and a digital camera.
- ✧ Be as quiet and unobtrusive as possible.
- ✧ Head out in the early morning for best bird-watching. The warmer the weather, the earlier you should head out.
- ✧ You'll see the most birds during spring and fall migration.
- ✧ Study up on the bird you want to spot, so you have a good idea of its behavior, appearance, sounds, and habitat.
- ✧ Steer clear of any nests.
- ✧ Be patient.

A NOTE ABOUT RABIES

Both people and animals can contract rabies, which is caused by a nasty virus that will spread through the body and kill if not treated quickly. You can prevent rabies with a vaccine; if you are bitten or scratched by a rabid beast, seek medical attention right away. You'll need several shots to kick it out of your system.

While you might typically think of a rabid animal as foaming at the mouth, signs may not be that obvious. They could be disoriented or acting strangely or display no visible signs. Any mammal, even the cute ones, can get or carry rabies. So, again, let's drive home the point that you should not feed, water, touch, or otherwise engage with any wildlife, no matter how tame it seems. And if it's dead, leave it be.

If you have been exposed to an animal's saliva, wash the wound for at least ten minutes with soap and water. Seek medical attention, and describe the animal as best you can. If your dog has been bitten or scratched, use gloves to clean your pet's wound. Hoof it to the vet's office and describe the attacking beast as best you can.

EPILOGUE: BETTY, THE WILDERNESS WONDER WOMAN

So, my dear, sweet, kick-ass Betty, you are ready to take on the great outdoors with style and aplomb. Remember your last dinner party and what a rousing success it was? That's *nothing* compared to your triumph in the backcountry. You tackled strenuous exercise outside of the gym, admired the beauty all around you even while burying your poo, tricked out your gear with a bit of Betty style, cooked up a meal that would win you immunity on *Top Chef*, feng shui-ed a comfortable campsite, and did it all while smelling like flowers (or at least nothing unpleasant).

Well-played, Betty. I'm not going to suggest that any of this is easy (although you make it look effortless). It takes constant diligence to go through the backcountry safely and responsibly, without disturbing nature, the ecosystem, or a hibernating griz-zly bear. And in the heat of the moment, it's easy to forget some basics, let alone expert information. So tuck this and any other guidebook into your pack when you head to the backcountry. And if you are unsure of anything, listen to your excellent instincts and err on the side of being overly cautious. It's better to pack too much than too little, to stretch longer and take an

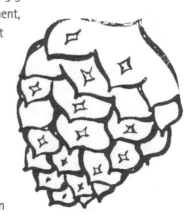

Advil at the first sign of joint pain, to tie your food up high, high, high, to snuggle up next to a warm body when it's cold, cold, cold. As I said, listen to your instincts and act accordingly. Even if you are camping by the "fake it 'til you make it" philosophy, your campanions will be wowed by your confidence and capability. They'll start to seriously wonder if you were lying when you said the closest you've gotten to the wild was that warehouse rave party last weekend.

To make sure you impress (and have the kind of backcountry experience you deserve), here's a handy recap to help you navigate your first trip into the wild. The most important thing to take with you is your style and moxie, which you already have in spades. Mmm, Kate Spade . . .

THE TOP TEN

While we've covered a lot of handy outdoor gear, there are ten essential things every Backcountry Betty needs to bring along on her rustic romp for wilderness survival, let alone an adventure that will make you keen to repeat the experience.

1. **Navigation.** While you may use a cabbie or your cell phone to navigate any city (411: "Hello, can you give me the address of Saks, please?"), you'll need different tools when you are off the grid. Namely, you should arm yourself with a map and compass. But first, you should learn how to read a map and use a compass. If you know you are heading north out of the parking lot, for instance, you'll know that you'll need to follow the compass's direction for south to make it back to your ride. Knowing the direction of the sun's path (rises in the east, sets in the west) and which side of a tree moss grows on (north side, at least in our part of the Northern Hemisphere) will also help you find your bearings.

2. **Sun protection.** Duh. As a Betty with gorgeous creamy skin, you are well aware of the importance of SPF. Pack a sturdy pair

of sunglasses (leave the logo shades in their protective case at home) and a serious sunscreen for both body and face. While you're at it, pack a hat to further protect your hair, scalp, and face. Now is not the time to tan. It will be uneven at best, and burned and blistered at worst.

3. **Insulation.** Pack layers of warm clothing. You can always peel off layers as you warm up, but if you don't have extra garments in your pack, you could be at risk for hypothermia. It can get cold up there in the mountains, and freak weather has been known to roll in quickly. And I hate to break it to you, but you can't turn up the thermostat or run into your bedroom for that snuggly cashmere throw on the end of your bed.

4. **Illumination.** No, not aromatherapy candles, silly! Fire is indeed a hazard and often illegal in the wild so maneuver through the darkness with moonlight, candle lanterns, a headlamp, and flashlight. While not the most stylish choice, a headlamp can leave your hands free to pursue some orchestral maneuvers in the dark.

5. **First-aid supplies.** No one anticipates cutting, burning, spraining, or otherwise injuring themselves, but it's been known to happen to the graceful and clumsy alike. So don't think you're exempt and leave your first-aid kit in your medicine cabinet. Pack antiseptic wipes, bandages, first-aid tape, gauze, small scissors, etc. I also like packing ibuprofen and moleskin.

6. **Fire starter.** In cold climates or nasty conditions, it may be necessary to seek shelter and build a fire. To that end, you'll need firestarter, such as cotton balls smeared with petroleum jelly or any alcohol-based product, and matches in a waterproof container or a lighter. All the kindling and dry firewood in the world won't help you if you can't ignite it.

7. **Repair kit and tools.** Leave the shoe polish and the make-up

bag at home. The kind of repair you might need to perform in the backcountry depends on your outing. Camping? Bring along extra fuel for your stove, tools for your tent, a good knife for any number of uses. If you are mountain biking, bring along an air pump and tools to repair your bike on the trail. Let your adventure dictate the kind of tools to bring along.

8. **Nutrition.** Don't rely on foraging fresh berries and delightful flora; bring along ample snacklets to get through at least one unexpected night. Protein bars, dried meat, and other packable items may be poor substitutes for the mesclun greens and glazed salmon on which you are used to dining. But a Betty is nothing if not resourceful, and in the wild, let's face it, everything tastes like four-star dining when you are ravenous. And as we talked about in chapter 3, there are lots of tasty options that don't take a lot of work, ingredients, or chef's kitchen.

9. **Hydration.** Drinking water will not only keep your skin glowing, it will keep you hydrated and, well, alive. At the minimum, pack 2 to 3 quarts of water per person per day. If you plan on getting water from a natural source (such as a freshwater stream), you must purify the water before drinking it, as there are a lot of critters and bacteria lurking in the liquid. Adding water purification tablets or using a water filter are the easiest methods. You can also boil your newly gathered water. Pour water through a clean cloth and boil for at least one minute. Allow to cool and store in a clean container.

10. **Emergency shelter.** I know you think of the outlet mall as emergency shelter but there are more important things afoot in the forest than retail therapy. Know how to pitch a tent, yes, but also identify suitable places to seek shelter in inclement weather or harsh terrain.

GLOSSARY

This is incomplete, as there is an entire language for outdoor enthusiasts. For more information, you can look online at various camping and outdoor sites.

acclimatization: The gradual process your body goes through as it gets used to high altitudes.

backcountry: Remote areas (like national parks and forests) with no paved roads or buildings, just uninhabited areas for Betties to explore.

backpacking: As you would expect, it means trekking into the backcountry with all of your gear on your—you guessed it—back.

bank, embankment: The part of the soil adjacent to a body of water that is higher than the water level.

base camp: The camp you set up where all-day trips and excursions start and end. It's the place you call home while you're in the wild, allowing you to dump heavy gear and go exploring with only the necessary items.

bear-bagging: Tying up your food securely at least ten feet high and four feet from tree trunks to protect it from bears and other critters.

biodegradable: Able to decompose without harming the environment.

bivouac: The site where you pitch your tent, or to spend a night outdoors without a tent.

bushwhack: Off-trail hiking. But as I've written, you should always stay to the marked, maintained trails.

cairn: A stacked pile of rocks used to mark a trail or route.

camping lantern: A portable light (with a handle) that is fueled by propane, kerosene, candles, or some other fuel.

camp stove: A portable cooking surface fueled by propane or another fuel source. A safe, environmentally sound way to rustle up your grub.

canopy: The leaf and branch cover in a forest.

car camping: A convenient way of camping that allows you to drive close to your campsite and carry your gear a short distance.

carabiner: An oblong metal clip with a spring-loaded lever used in rock climbing.

cat hole: A preferred method for depositing your waste. Dig a hole six to eight inches deep, do your business, and cover it when finished. Should be located at least 200 feet from water and from your campsite.

compass: A magnetic device that aids in determining your position or directing your way. Usually used with a map.

day pack: A small pack that allows you to carry food, water, and supplies for a day hike.

dehydration: An excessive loss of body fluids.

Dutch oven: A cast-iron cooking pot (with lid) for cooking one-pot meals. Can place oven over charcoals or bury it in the earth under hot coals.

elevation: The height of a place, measured in number of feet above sea level.

fauna: The animals of a specific area.

feng shui: The Chinese art and science of arranging spaces and elements to create harmonious energy flows and patterns. Yes, you can feng shui your campsite.

fire pan: A pan with a three-inch lip that allows you to have a fire in the wilderness without causing harm to the soil or environment.

fire ring: Circle of rocks used to contain a campfire. Only use in designated, legal areas.

flora: The plants of a specific area.

foil dinner: A meal cooked entirely in foil on a camp stove or over a fire.

four-season tent: A tent that can be used year-round; it's built for wear, harsh weather, and winter.

frostbite: Exposure to freezing temperatures resulting in tissue death, numbness, and gangrene in the extremities.

Gore-Tex: A water-repellent, breathable material used in outdoor clothing and gear.

GPS: Global positioning system uses satellite triangulation to fix on your exact position.

grade: The amount of elevation change between two points over a given distance. It is expressed as a percentage. For instance, a trail can have a 10 percent grade if it rises 10 vertical feet every 100 horizontal feet. Sounds like a nightmare story problem from ninth grade, doesn't it?

ground cover: Vegetation that spreads out, covers, and protects the soil.

heat exhaustion: When the body overheats, and not in a good "Clive Owen was in my dreams" way. Symptoms include salt deficiency and dehydration.

heat stroke: Also called sunstroke, a more severe form of heat exhaustion brought on by extreme temperatures and dehydration.

hypothermia: A condition usually occurring in cold, wet, or frigid temperatures, where your body loses more heat than it generates and your body temperature dips dangerously low.

kindling: Small pieces of downed dry wood used to start a fire.

land ethic: The desire to conserve, protect, and respect the native landscape and other natural resources.

latrine: A communal, reusable temporary toilet dug near a campsite for use by all campanions.

leave no trace (LNT): Educational program designed to instill behaviors in the outdoors that leave minimum impact of human activities or occupation. In other words, leave the place just like you found it.

lyme disease: An infection caused by a bacteria carried by pesky deer ticks. Early symptoms include fever, headache, stiffness, and lethargy. See a doctor immediately if you suspect you have the disease.

mineral soil: Layers of the subsoil that are mostly free of organic matter.

mound fire: A way to safely make a fire in the wilderness by building a small fire in a hollowed-out mound of dirt.

mummy bag: A narrow sleeping bag that is tapered at the ends for maximum heat conservation.

organic soil: Soil comprising leaves, needles, plants, roots, bark, and other organic material in various stages of decay.

poison ivy, poison oak, poison sumac: Pesky plants that can cause a nasty rash when the skin comes into contact with them.

polypropylene: Cool outdoorsy people refer to this fabric as "polypro." One of the very first man-made wicking materials, polypro wicks sweat away from the skin and some newer versions of the fabric even deal with body odor effectively. Proprietary brands include Capilene and MTS 2 (Moisture Transport System).

potable water: Water that is safe to drink without treating.

rabies: An infectious disease transmitted by the saliva of an infected mammal (and yep, bats are mammals). Symptoms include headache, fever, loss of appetite, fatigue, abdominal pain, nausea, vomiting, and diarrhea. If bitten by a rabid or wild mammal, seek medical attention immediately.

radiant heat loss: Heat radiates out from your body into your clothes, which reflect the heat back to your body. Great in colder weather; height of summer, not so much.

sight distance: Basically, the area you can see ahead of you and behind you from any point on the trail.

sleeping bag: A roll-up, zip-up bed made of various insulating materials to keep you snug and cozy at your campsite.

sleeping pad: An extra insulating cushion you place under your sleeping bag for added comfort and warmth.

spelunking: Exploring caves or caverns.

stuff sack: A lightweight, water-repellent drawstring bag used to carry a tent or camping gear.

switchback: A sharp turn to reverse the direction of travel and to gain elevation on a trail.

tarp: Waterproof or laminated canvas shelter or dropcloth.

three-season tent: A tent built for spring, summer, and fall.

trail: A land or water route that is protected and provides public access for recreation and transportation.

trail marker: A sign of some sort used to mark a route.

trailhead: The entry point to a trail or trail system, often accompanied by various public facilities, such as restrooms, water, and a map.

tree line: The highest altitude at which trees are able to grow. Beyond this line, the environment is too harsh for trees to survive. When looking at a mountain from a distance, you can usually see its tree line. When hiking past the tree line, know that the air is becoming thin and the conditions harsher.

trekking pole(s): Sort of like ski poles, these hiking poles can reduce fatigue, increase speed, and provide stability while hiking.

ventilation: Methods of removing body moisture inside your tent or clothing. Vents, mesh, and special wicking fabrics can aid in ventilation.

water resistant: The ability to resist water. Water resistant items are not completely waterproof, however.

waterproof: As you would expect, since you're a smart girl, something that is waterproof can completely repel water.

wicking: Pulling sweat away from the surface of your skin and transferring or distributing it into other clothing layers. This keeps you dry and comfortable in the summer, and warm in colder weather. Always look for outdoor clothing with wicking properties.

wilderness: Undeveloped land and water resources that retain their uncultivated, original character.

wildlife: Any undomesticated animal species living in its natural habitat. Never touch or feed the wildlife while visiting the backcountry.

RESOURCES

Books

McGivney, Annette, *Leave No Trace: A Practical Guide to the New Wilderness Etiquette.* Seattle: The Mountaineers Books, 1998.

Van Tilburg, Christopher, M.D., ed. *Emergency Survival: A Pocket Guide: Quick Information for Outdoor Safety.* Seattle: The Mountaineers Books, 2001.

Van Tilburg, Christopher, M.D., ed. *First Aid: A Pocket Guide: Quick Information for Mountaineering and Backcountry Use.* Seattle: The Mountaineers Books, 2001.

Websites

ACTIVITIES

ABC of Rock Climbing: *www.abc-of-rockclimbing.com*

American Birding Association: *www.americanbirding.org*

Audubon: *www.audubon.org*

Becky's Campfire Songbook: *www.dragon.sleepdeprived.ca/songbook /songbook_index.htm*

Bird-watching: *www.birdwatching.com*

The MacScouter—Scouting Resources Online: *www.macscouter .com/Songs/CampfireSongs.html*

The National Spelogical Society: *www.caves.org*

Raftinfo.com, an online directory of white-water rafting outfitters: *www.raftinfo.com*

ScoutSongs.com Virtual Songbook: *www.scoutsongs.com*

Swimming Holes: *www.swimmingholes.org*

White-water Rafting in North America: *www.e-raft.com*

APPAREL AND GEAR

Coleman: The Outdoor Company: *www.coleman.com*
Lucy, women's activewear apparel and accessories: *www.lucy.com*
lululemon athletica: *www.lululemon.com*
Marmot for Life: *www.marmot.com*
REI: *www.REI.com*
Title 9 Sports: *www.titlenine.com*
UnderArmour Performance Women's Sportswear:
    www.underarmour.com

MISCELLANEOUS

AlpineAire Foods: *www.alpineaire.com*
American Trails: *www.americantrails.org*
Backpacker's Pantry: *www.backpackerspantry.com*
Leave No Trace: Center for Outdoor Ethics: *www.lnt.org*
UDAP Bear Deterrent: *www.udap.com*